LEADING THROUGH THE CROSSFIRE

I0093292

A Veteran's Blueprint for Navigating
Toxic Work Environments

LT. COL. JASON G. PIKE, USA, RETIRED

ISBN Paperback: 979-8-9889610-2-4
ISBN Electronic: 979-8-9889610-3-1
Library of Congress Control Number: Need

Publishing Consultant: PRESStinely - PRESStinely.com

Portions of this book are works of nonfiction. Certain names and identifying characteristics have been changed.

Printed in the United States of America.

Lt. Col. Jason G. Pike, USA, Retired
JasonPike.org

DISCLAIMER
Although this publication is designed to provide accurate information regarding the subject matter covered, the publisher and the author assume no responsibility for errors, inaccuracies, omissions, or any other inconsistencies herein. This publication is meant as a source of valuable information for the reader; however, it is not meant as a replacement for direct expert assistance. If such a level of assistance is required, the services of a competent professional should be sought.

TABLE OF CONTENTS

ACKNOWLEDGEMENTS

I could not have written this book without the invaluable input and advice from the following incredible people.

Peter Baxter

Major Chris Lang
Active Duty, USA (United States Army)

COL George E Reed, PhD
USA retired, Dean and Professor, University of Colorado, Colorado Springs

COL Jack Wedam
USA retired, Author

COL Jennifer Caci
USA retired

MSgt Steven Nisbet
United States Air Force retired, Pararescueman

Bryan Davis
Author, Zine maker, Photographer, Husband, Cat lover

Susan Gold
Author

Dr. Edward Evans
Retired Department of the Army leader/employee

Kathy Mullin

Cynthia Douglas-Ybarra

LTC Ray Paul Santillano
United States Army Duty

Ashlie Walton, MBA

Trauma Recovery Coach, PCC Life Coach, PCC Mentor Coach

LEO Warriors, LLC

INTRODUCTION

We tried to put the war on trial, but the military court said the truth is no defense

Howard Levy

IN JANUARY 2023, I PUBLISHED a memoir of my thirty-one-year career in the United States Military. It surprised me a little bit when, during the subsequent promotion, most of the interest generated around the book concerned my experiences with toxic leadership. Although this was not the central theme of the book, it certainly did seem to make the most impression on a whole lot of people. I guess my experience was not unique. I understand now that a lot of folks out there, perhaps most of them, in and out of uniform, have had to deal at some time with corrosive leadership. There is a good amount of literature out there too, dealing with the subject, most of it originating from military sources, which tells me that the issue is recognized and understood and that a serious effort is underway to address it.

The statistics vary, depending on the source, but even the military itself will admit that a majority of men and women in uniform have experienced toxic leadership at some level, with a significant percentage admitting that they thought seriously about ending their careers because of it. Matter of fact, I know several junior officers who have left the military because of toxic leadership. Bad leadership has driven people to suicide, and in fact, the experience of toxic or corrosive leadership is at the root of more post-traumatic stress than combat. Once I got to talking to folk about it, I was astonished at how pervasive it is.

At different times during my career, I found myself on just about every side of this issue. In the first instance, I became the subject of a concerted campaign, by one senior officer in particular, to discredit my name and standing in the 18th MEDCOM in Korea. As this book progresses I will probably talk a lot about that. Then, during my first combat command in Afghanistan, I had to mediate on behalf of a female sergeant who was the subject of constant attacks from a toxic captain, who was actually my executive officer. I also led an investigation into an anonymous whistleblower report while I was on assignment with the Defense Logistics Agency. So I have certainly had my fair share of experience in this area, maybe more than most, and that got me to thinking.

When it was happening to me, I had no idea that there were resources and procedures out there to help, and counseling services to relieve some of the isolation of being on some crazy commanders shitlist. Most of what I subsequently read about it was either in reports, directives, or academic studies, with nothing that the common soldier would find accessible. I figured it would have helped me a lot to know more about it, and how to deal with it, but there is so much damn anxiety involved with being under investigation that I probably would not have understood what to do anyway, and that was the beginning of my thought process on this book.

The institution with the most dynamic leadership hierarchy and structure is obviously the military, but toxic and destructive leadership is a fact of life wherever there is a departmental organization, or where individuals work together under any sort of hierarchical system. Human nature is flawed, ego and ambition are perennial phenomena, and where personal advancement serves as the primary imperative, oppression, conflict and discontent in the ranks are inevitable.

In 2010, Professor of Anthropology, David Matsuda, was commissioned by the military to investigate why some thirty U.S. soldiers stationed in Iraq committed suicide in the previous year. The results of that investigation revealed that, while most, if not all of those soldiers suffered significant problems in their personal lives, the one single common denominator was that they had each complained of a leader that made their lives hell. This set a ball in motion in the corridors of military administration, bringing, for the first time, the issue of toxic leadership in the ranks of uniformed services into the full light of day. In 2012, for the first time, the military attempted to define toxic leadership, and this was the result:

Toxic leadership is a combination of self-centered attitudes, motivations, and behaviors that have adverse effects on subordinates, the organization, and mission performance. This leader lacks concern for others and the climate of the organization, which leads to short- and long-term negative effects. The toxic leader operates with an inflated sense of self-worth and acute self-interest. Toxic leaders consistently use dysfunctional behaviors to deceive, intimidate, coerce, or unfairly punish others to get what they want for themselves. The negative leader completes short-term requirements by operating at the bottom of the continuum of commitment, where followers respond to the positional power of their leader to fulfill requests. This may achieve results in the short term but ignores the other leader competency categories of leads and development. Prolonged use of negative leadership to influence followers undermines the followers' will, initiative, and potential and destroys unit morale.[1]

---

[1] Army Doctrine 6—22

Well done to the military for that, and they do say that ninety percent of solving a problem is identifying a problem. However, although there can be no doubt that the military establishment in this country has made it a priority to *try* and solve this issue, it is proving to be very difficult. Various studies suggest that some ten to thirty percent of personnel in leadership positions within the military are toxic, which, on the one hand, is quite a modest percentage, but on the other, those that are toxic are usually in a position to have a disproportionate impact on unit health, and the long term effectiveness of their various commands.

As quite a few people remarked to me in the many conversations I had in preparation for writing this book, toxic leadership in the military seems to revolve around a cycle of destructive leaders, susceptible followers, and a conducive environment. It is a fact that poor leadership is allowed to survive because of the willing or unwilling complicity of subordinates, and because the military hierarchy is inclined to reward aggressive, ambitious, competent, and high-achieving individuals simply because they do get the job done, and for that reason, they always tend to look good on paper.

So far, the military has been surprisingly creative in trying to break that cycle. Today there are many different avenues by which an individual, or group of soldiers, can draw attention to issues at a command level. There are also ideas like 360-degree evaluations, which imply that evaluations are not just top-down, whereby commanders evaluate their subordinates, but also subordinates evaluating their commanders.

I know that when I was still in uniform they had a system where you had to get people from your left and right as well as your subordinates to evaluate you. I was processing out of the military at that time so I am not certain how it all evolved. I do know that you can pull in buddies to give you a good evaluation. The jury is still out over the question of how effective the 360-degree evaluation idea is, but what is certain is that the Army is at least trying.

In this book, we will take a deep dive into the issue of toxic leadership in the military, on the understanding that the essential dynamic involved overlaps into the corporate and administrative worlds, and that similar causes and effects are experienced. The various causes and characteristics of toxic leadership will be discussed in the first part of this book, after which we'll take a look at several possible ways subordinates can mitigate the issues of toxic leadership. We will share the stories of a few individuals who have dealt with this phenomenon, and with some luck, we'll offer a few answers for those currently dealing with it.

THE PRICE OF MUTINY

Military justice wants discipline – that is, action in obedience to regulations and orders; this being absolutely necessary for prompt, competent, and decisive handling of masses of men

John Henry Wigmore

ONE OF THE FIRST THINGS I FIGURED out as I got into the weeds of this issue is that confronting leadership in the military is a risky business because the playing field is tilted very conspicuously in favor of the leadership establishment. Throughout history, mutinies, be they on land or the high seas, have tended to be very rare. Much of the reason for this lies in the fact that the system is stacked so heavily against the mutineers, in particular, if the issue finds its way to a court martial. Why is insubordination so sternly regarded in the uniformed ranks? I ran that question by an old friend who has a lot of experience in dealing with probes and investigations related to leadership, and this was his reply:

"The deck is heavily stacked against any soldier who has a mind to challenge the leader, and the reason is primarily to ensure good order and discipline in the heat of battle, which is a time when a lot of soldiers can be expected to start having second thoughts. The system is geared, not for the survival of the *individual*, but of the *unit*. If a commander has to make a snap decision to throw one group of soldiers onto the flank to defend the unit, knowing they will probably be killed, discipline must be strong enough that those soldiers will obey, despite understanding the likely result. There are provisions for challenging that decision later, but in the heat of the battle, when people are afraid for their lives, discipline must hold for the greater good of the unit. The system cannot, and does not, reflect kindly on soldiers who question an order in the heat of battle."

There have been many incidences of justified mutiny being rewarded with capital punishment. The *Mutiny on the Bounty* is probably the most famous, and Captain Bligh is one of the most toxic leaders in the entire span of British maritime history. At a time when ships of the Royal Navy were scattered across the seven seas, out of direct communication with one another and central headquarters in London, the authority of captains had, by necessity, to be almost god-like. Regardless of how justified a mutiny might be, the mutineers could expect to be hung if they were caught, as a general lesson to rank and file. In France, in 1917, during the awful attrition of trench warfare, a series of famous mutinies broke out in protest against the mass casualties sustained in the kind of set-piece advances that characterized the Great War. More than 3,000 courts-martial were held, and 629 sentences of death passed. Soldiers expected to climb over the top, and walk in formation into the face of ranks of German machine guns, could not be granted an inch of leeway to object. It was death in the face of the enemy, or death in front of a firing squad.

Those sorts of behaviors do not occur today, at least not in the ranks of a modern, constituted army. What was once regarded as cowardice, punishable by death, is now more accurately linked to the trauma of exposure to combat conditions, and is dealt with not by a Sergeant Major leading a firing squad, but by a psychological examination conducted by a medical expert. Nonetheless, the moral of the story is simply that insubordination in the ranks of the uniformed services, especially in a time of war, requires sound evidence, and a very strong case to justify.

The U.S. Uniformed Code of Military Justice was inherited almost verbatim from British military law, which was in turn derived from Roman military law. Roman military law was the first law codified specifically to deal with military issues, and it shows that, 2,000 years ago, the Romans were dealing with most of the same kinds of problems that we do today. Under Roman orders, soldiers were rigorously disciplined and severely punished if they ran foul of the accepted code of conduct. Insubordination, regardless of circumstance, was an act of treason, the worst of all crimes, and the horrifying punishments that it attracted were a powerful incentive for the rank and file to remain loyal. In the 17th century, the English adopted a series of *Articles of War*, based on those Roman provisions, which were adopted more or less letter-perfect by the new republic of the United States. In 1775, with a vote of the Second Continental Congress, the first Continental Army was established, which immediately demanded some sort of basis of military law. Sixty-nine *Articles of War* were proposed, based on prevailing British and colonial law. These articles, which were ratified by Congress on June 30, 1775, codified numerous offenses that might be tried by court-martial, including insubordination, which was potentially punishable by death.

The modern Uniform Code of Military Justice, which came into effect in 1950, still contains many of those original provisions, with the main adjustment being the 'Uniform' aspect of the code. This does not bear reference to 'uniforms' as the distinguishing aspect of the military, but rather it implies a uniform or standardized system of law for all branches of the military. Before 1950, each of the various services functioned under their own particular systems of law, mostly parallel, but not unified. Again, among what is known as the punitive articles, can be found Article 90, which states that any person who – '...*willfully disobeys a lawful command of his superior commissioned officer*', shall be punished, if the offense is committed in a time of war, by death, or such other punishment as a court-martial shall direct.[1]

Death, in this instance, was probably quite rare, but the sentiment reaches back deep into history, and the routine decimation of a Roman cohort guilty of capital offenses, such as cowardice, mutiny, desertion, or insubordination. The Romans were no less aware than we are today that if discipline breaks down in the ranks of armed forces, wars will be lost, and nations will descend into chaos.

This leads us to the question of why a specific system of law to govern the military, separate from civilian law, was considered necessary in the first place, and why was it immediately essential for the officer corps of the new Continental Army to include a class of lawyers. According to the US Supreme Court, the military is an organization unique and separate from civilian society, with laws and traditions of its own, dating back many, many years. This issue was examined in a very interesting Supreme Court judgment in the case of Parker v. Levy in 1974. In an opinion delivered by Justice Rehnquist, one of many observations ran as follows:

"An army is not a deliberative body. It is the executive arm. *Its law is that of obedience*. No question can be left open as to the right to command in the officer or the duty of obedience in the soldier."

---

[1] UCMJ §895. Art. 95. *Offenses by Sentinel or Lookout*

The Parker v. Levy case is probably a good one to dwell on briefly as we get into the nuts and bolts of this matter. That is because it speaks to the issue of the higher moral instruction of a conscientious objector and the implications of a refusal to obey an order regarded as contrary to an individual's moral code. Although conscientious objectors have always occupied a very maligned place in military lore, the fact that there have been so few of them speaks to how effective the military is at breaking down and replacing the individual with the collective. The team is ultimately, and always will be, of greater significance than the individual. When that principle dissolves, so too does the universal concept of the military.

Howard Levy was a US Army doctor who was court-martialed in 1967 for refusing an order to train Green Beret medics in preparation for service in Vietnam. He reasoned that the skills imparted would be used to win Vietnamese hearts and minds, while at the same time, the iron fist of the military was being used to victimize Vietnamese villagers in search and destroy missions. He regarded the US Special Forces as "killers of peasants and murderers of women and children." The late 1960s were the peak of operations in Vietnam, and in 1968, it was the notorious My Lai Massacre that came to dominate the news cycle stateside. We will touch on that episode as well.

Levy's defense leaned heavily on the Nuremberg principle, which was simply that the plea of "I was just following orders" does not automatically shield an individual from culpability in war crimes. Levy also called on black troops to refuse service in Vietnam, thanks to general discrimination against them and the fact that they were sustaining far greater numbers of casualties. Ultimately, the court-martial was found against Howard Levy, and he was sentenced to three years at Leavenworth for "conduct unbecoming of an officer".

The case then went through the appeal process, attracting huge attention, and becoming a lightning rod for resistance to the Vietnam War. His conviction was confirmed by a Federal District Court, overturned by the United States Court of Appeals, and ultimately reinstated by the Supreme Court in the now famous Parker v. Levy decision. It was that decision, delivered by Justice William Rehnquist, that remains the legal foundation for the understanding that "military necessity" carries more weight than the First Amendment rights of individuals in the military.

The story that this tells, at least for our purposes, is that military service personnel function under a system of law that is separate and different from the principal law of the land. The system is stacked against the mutineer, and if push comes to shove, the civilian branches of law will come down on the side of the military. And the reason for that is, once again, that the military establishment can only exist through *unquestioning* loyalty to the chain of command. The reason that I make such a point of emphasizing this is for it to be understood that taking a stand against the monolithic edifice of the military establishment can not only be a very lonely quest, but also one that is almost preconditioned to fail.

It is probably also worth bearing in mind that very few leadership issues are as dramatic as this, but the principle remains the same. One of the motivating factors behind Howard Levy's solitary protest was the My Lai Massacre, which tested this principle in the fires of war. Most men and women in uniform today are familiar with this episode, but for those that are not, the essential details are this:

On March 16, 1968, a search and destroy mission in a coastal district of South Vietnam went awry, to the extent that a company of US infantry killed, many say *murdered*, upwards of 340 Vietnamese civilians. That was the My Lai massacre, arguably the darkest stain on the professional reputation of the US Army. Many women and young girls were raped, and a significant number of the dead were children. When the question is asked – "What happened to allow this atrocity to occur?" – the finger is typically pointed at a breakdown in leadership and a failure of the chain of command.

There have been more books written about this issue than can be listed here, and there is not much about the episode that has not been dissected and studied. Concerning command failure, the most common theme is that it was the rotational policy of the Army that ultimately undermined command effectiveness. It was said at the time that – "The Americans don't have ten years experience in Vietnam; they have one year's experience repeated ten times over." A majority of battalion and brigade commanders were rotated into, and out of command positions on average every six months, so that everyone should have an opportunity to command. To check the box. Each time a new commander came in for his six-month tour, the effectiveness of the chain of command was reset.

However, for a unit of ostensibly trained and disciplined men to run so amok, and wreak such absolute horror, has to have a deeper explanation. The unit involved had been in combat for three months, and had suffered significant casualties, but had yet to gain the satisfaction of an open fight with the Viet Cong. Most of their casualties had been caused by snipers and booby traps, and a significant amount of frustration and anger was building up in the unit, and the ranks. Possibly this, and an inexperienced platoon leader in the form of 2nd Lieutenant William Calley, who was himself quite obviously caught up in the passion and bloodlust of the moment, explains much of what happened on that day.

As the story goes, Lieutenant Calley was a mediocre officer, perhaps not a toxic leader in the sense implied by this book, but a weak and ineffective twenty-four-year-old, unemployed when he entered the Army, and a low achieving Officer Candidate School graduate. He was small in stature, generally disrespected by the men of his platoon, and with a whole lot to prove after just three months in-country. Had his moral compass been more correctly aligned, Calley would have compensated for command and planning failures by ordering a halt to the unlawful killings underway all around him. It seems, however, that he lacked the character and authority to influence his platoon at that moment, and in any case, he appeared to be completely caught up in the madness himself and was personally responsible for many of the killings.

The hero of the story was a helicopter reconnaissance pilot by the name of Warrant Officer Hugh Thompson, who saw what was taking place, queried it with higher command, and then intervened directly to protect Vietnamese civilians. He ordered his tech and door gunner to open fire on American troops if they attempted to kill any civilians under his protection. In his account of the episode, Thomson recalls a confrontation with Calley where the latter commented that he was just following orders, that it was his business, and that Thomson should just get out of the way and do his job, leaving the platoon to do their job.

Later that day, Hugh Thompson submitted a report through the chain of command, at a point when the seriousness of what had taken place at My Lai was beginning to be generally appreciated. While similar operations were promptly halted, and although

Thompson was interviewed in some detail by Colonel Oran Henderson, the issue was effectively covered up.

And so it remained until, some months later, privately taken color images surfaced in *Life Magazine*. In late 1969, Hugh Thompson was summoned to Washington DC to appear before a special closed hearing of the House Armed Services Committee, and there he was sharply criticized by various congressmen, in particular Chairman Mendel Rivers, who were anxious to downplay any allegations of a massacre by American troops. In fact, Chairman Rivers stated publicly that he felt Thompson was the only soldier at My Lai who deserved punishment, for turning his weapons on fellow American troops, and he tried, unsuccessfully, to have Thompson court-martialed.

The moral of the story is that Hugh Thomson was universally vilified, not only by the military establishment but by the public at large. Fourteen officers were eventually charged by court-martial for crimes related to the massacre, but most of those charges were later dropped. Throughout proceedings, William Calley, by then a captain, claimed that he was just following orders. He was, however, found guilty of the premeditated murder of some twenty people, convicted, and sentenced to life in prison. Clearly, he took the fall for a lot of other guilty people up the chain of command who slipped through the net. Ultimately, he would serve just forty-two months under house arrest at Fort Benning, in what can only be regarded as a token punishment. Punished far more harshly was Hugh Thompson, whose name thereafter was dirt, and whose career was permanently damaged. A heavy price to pay for drawing attention to a monumental failure of leadership.

THE BOTTOM LINE HERE, once again, is that the system, at the very least, is stacked against the man who blows the whistle on leadership failures, and the decision to do so is not one to be taken lightly. The military is a strange animal, and as my friend also said, "There are no career privates." In other words, within the rank structure of the military, every individual at some point or another will find his or herself in a leadership position, regardless of merit, and so inevitably, in such a vast and hierarchical organization, a lot of poor leaders will end up commanding soldiers. In my conversations with people in preparation for putting pen to paper on this book, I encountered so many situations where competent and well-intentioned people were diminished and demoralized by poor leadership, and at times by aggressively destructive leadership, many without any clear sense of how to deal with it. I know I did not know how to deal with it when I saw it. I hope, in these pages, that we will shed a bit of light on the phenomenon, and offer a few solutions.

A Few Initial Thoughts

All too often, these bullies feel justified for their actions against victims. Since they can do no wrong (in their own minds), the victim is the problem, and the bullies feel justified in their persecution.

Ronald E. Riggio

MY PERSONAL EXPERIENCE of toxic leadership was amplified, I believe, by the improbability of my reaching an 'O' paygrade, the officer pay grade, at all. It is somewhat rare for an enlisted soldier to be commissioned anyway, but for someone of my background, and with my diagnosed learning disabilities, it is almost unheard of. Just by way of background, I signed up for the South Carolina National Guard at the age of seventeen to get a college education. The National Guard is a reserve force. We were a less-than-best organization at that time. None of my friends, family, or school counselors encouraged me to consider college. My SAT scores, and my college entrance test, were very low, so they had logic to believe this. But I did go to college, and now I hold a bachelor`s and two master`s degrees. Because I was a college degree holder, I was commissioned through the ROTC program at Clemson University. However, when Uncle Sam picks up the tab for college, a more active commitment is required, and that is how, and why, I entered the professional ranks of the United States Army.

I began my active duty career with the 10th Special Forces Group at Fort Devens in Massachusetts, and there I felt right at home. Although I was a staff officer, a chemical officer, in fact, and not a green beret, I still dropped into that environment like a fish into the water. The reason is that this environment is very unconventional. I enjoyed it very much. My mannerisms and my crude, less-than-best behavior were not frowned upon, nor looked down on, but celebrated. At the time, Special Forces was still primarily a male environment, and I guess it still is, and a lot of the crude behaviors that go along with male fraternities, like farting, belching and scratching, drew no comment at all. Standards of day-to-day discipline were lower, and informality was the rule. I eventually transferred out of the Special Forces, into preventive medicine. I found in preventive medicine that there were a lot more females involved.

My first deployment was to Korea, to a preventive medicine unit, and there were a lot of females there, and that is where I ran into trouble. Some reading this, who are familiar with that story, will probably suspect that I represented another facet of toxicity, which is not toxic leadership, but toxic subordinates. I ran into trouble for being a little bit too relaxed within the chain of command, more than a little irresponsible at times, and sometimes maybe thoughtless in my day-to-day interactions with the female NCOs, who made up much of the staff. I was pulled in by my commanding officer to be reminded that I was a preventive medicine officer, not a special forces officer anymore and that I could not walk into the office and rip a fart, dig in my ass, or belch loudly after drinking a Coke or something.

They called it 'gender insensitivity', which meant that the women in the office were offended. They were probably also offended by the fact that I was having an affair with a married local Korean woman who worked in the office and that I was known to be traveling fairly regularly to the Philippines for the same reason that most GIs flocked to the Philippines. I'm sure they also disliked my down-home southern manners and attitude and wished I could be more sensitive.

None of it was too serious, and all that happened in the end was that I shipped out under a cloud, probably to the relief of both my subordinates and superiors. The worst that could be said was that the women in the office hated me, and the commanding officer was irritated to have to deal with it. I was senior to most of those women, so was *I* a toxic leader? I guess at the time I probably could have been, but I would learn my lesson throughout the next couple of years when I got a DUI while on training at Fort Sam Houston and had to move heaven and earth to get that off my record. I learned a lot of real valuable lessons then and emerged as a better soldier, a better man, and certainly a better officer.

However, it was on my second and third deployments to South Korea that I saw a lot more toxic leadership. On my third deployment to South Korea, the shit hit the fan, and it had everything to do with a turf war within one of the mini-fiefdoms that riddle the military command structure. A lot of the dynamics in this situation were the same as the last – the elitism of the field ranks offended by someone like me with rough manners, kind of an insurgent senior officer somehow escaped from the enlisted ranks – and a desire, because of that, to get rid of me.

Because a senior officer is so difficult to get rid of under any circumstances, the method often applied is to create an unholy stink around that officer's reputation, justly or unjustly, generating such discomfort that that officer will either resign or apply for redeployment. It is a damned minefield, very difficult to spot in advance, and very difficult to get out of once you are in. It is about vague and unprovable accusations, wicked enough that they get the attention of higher folks above you, but without any identifiable source, but kept on the boil using rumor and innuendo. In the end, it is often not about the validity of any accusations, but just the accusations themselves. The power lies only in the accusation.

THE CURRENT, DEFINING TREATISE on toxic leadership is *Tarnished: Toxic Leadership in the US Military*, written by George Reed. In this chapter, I am going to devote some time to passing on a few of the thoughts and lessons I picked up from reading *Tarnished*, and later, from a few conversations that I had with George Reed.

At the time of writing, George Reed was Dean of the School of Public Affairs at the University of Colorado, Colorado Springs. According to his bio, he served twenty-seven years as an officer in the US Army, including six as the Director of Command and Leadership studies at the US Army War College. In the preface of his book, George Reed makes a point that I think is worth keeping at the forefront of our minds as we get deeper into this subject.

"I did not write this book because I was abused as a lieutenant." He wrote. "All lieutenants are abused at some point or another, and we took it all in our stride as the way things were. I experienced far more exemplary leadership than bad over my twenty-seven years in the army. Perhaps that is why the few bad ones stand out so vividly in my memory."[2]

I believe this to be true as well. The general leadership quality in the uniformed services of the United States is outstanding. However, although toxic leadership

---

[2] Reed, George E.. *Tarnished: Toxic Leadership in the U.S. Military* (Toxic Leadership in the Military) . Potomac Books. Kindle Edition.

is the exception rather than the rule, because of its destructive effects, it tends to be very visible. It is also sometimes difficult to sift out who are the good and who are the bad. Readers of this book who have also read my memoir will recall my reflections on Basic Training, and the methodology applied by my Drill Sergeant, William Ellenburg, to bring me, and a couple of other low-performing privates, up to speed.

In those days, I had no metric to determine what good or bad leadership looked like. I entered basic training, the same as every other recruit, and stepped completely blind into a world of hell. The screaming and shouting, the belittlement, and verbal abuse were coming in from every direction. Our minds were in such a haze of confusion that who in the hell could figure out, and who in the hell even cared, who were the good and who were the bad. We were just trying to survive. They all seemed like malicious, abusive little Hitlers, willfully maltreating a bunch of soft-bodied high schoolers. Sure, there were probably a few who were drunk on their power, but in most cases, there was a solid, tried-and-tested logic behind their madness.

William Ellenburg was an Army drill sergeant of the standard pattern. He was, and probably still is, short, fit, and compact, with a parade ground yell like a force-ten gale, and I understand exactly why he wasted no time in identifying me as a candidate to be smoked out of the platoon. That is a well-tested drill sergeant's method, intended on the one hand to weed out the lame, the lazy, and the crazy, and on the other to motivate the rest of the platoon. Ellenburg had his methods, and while he skated on pretty damn thin ice sometimes, he knew what he was doing.

This story doesn't happen in the Army, but it happened to me. Along with a couple of other low-achievers, I was checked into the Criminal Correction Facility, or CCF, for only about four hours. There we were smoked hard in a kind of *very* unofficial 'scared straight' strategy. Although we were severely punished for those four hours, what made the biggest impression was the belly crawl over hot gravel. That was rough, and we made big rocks into small rocks. We were in a criminal confinement facility – some people call it Charlie's chicken farm – and what he was trying to do was either make us or break us. More importantly, what he was trying to do was show us up as guinea pigs to the entire platoon, that if you don't make progress you'll come back looking like sorry Private Pike. That was tough love, and it was hell.

This CCF treatment was what I call a 'drug deal' between the drill sergeants at the time. They all sorta knew each other, and it would be easy for Ellenburg to just pick up the phone and arrange it. Maybe it happened often. I don't know. Either way, it was very extreme, but it worked. I came out of that experience energized, and determined not to be broken, and to his credit, Ellenburg picked up on the change immediately. Suddenly, his attitude shifted. Instead of trying to weed me out of the unit, he began to try and help me. By the end of basic training, I was the highest-scoring recruit, and most improved private of the entire platoon, and Ellenburg even announced that to the other guys in the platoon. He called me into his office one time. He asked me if I was crazy and needed medical help. I told him no, I was fine, and just needed more training. After that, he was on my side.

I recently came across a great article, published in the 2013 *Military Review*, entitled *Narcissism and Toxic Leaders*. In that article, the point is made: "As long as the imagined view of a successful leader (whether it is true or not) remains the screaming, yelling, selfish, berating commander standing in front of a soldier or a staff, then it is not likely that we will remove this cultural aspect from our services."

Well, hell, Ellenburg did nothing else than scream, yell, and berate soldiers. He was a hard, tough, and uncompromising sonofabitch, but he was by no means a toxic leader. He was an exemplary drill sergeant who forged a credible soldier out of a complete screw-up, and I owe him for that.

I guess what that tells me is that there is no rule of thumb. The same behavior perpetrated by two different people can have completely different effects. It just depends on the person.

One time, during jump training at Fort Devens, Massachusetts, while I was with the 10th Special Forces, the squad was scheduled to do a water jump. A water jump is a very technical exercise and usually requires a low-level approach. The training doctrine on this is rock solid, and it states that a trainee must *always* turn into the wind. The logic of that is to damp down speed and help achieve a better and more controlled landing.

As we were forming up, and for whatever reason, the jump master, a particular major, approached me and ordered me, and only me, to follow him, and turn *away* from the wind. That was the wrong thing to do. I knew it. I asked him about this, and he affirmed the order, and since I was only a young lieutenant at the time, and just a five-jump-chump, I did as I was ordered. This is how I described the episode in my memoir:

"We jumped, and while everyone tacked into the wind when their chutes opened, he and I broke ranks and turned away from the wind. We started hauling ass. This created instant consternation on the water. I looked down and saw the inflatable zodiacs arcing away and speeding up the lake to intercept us. When I saw that, I knew I was in trouble. We were coming down at high speed, moving away from the rest of the group, and bearing down on the opposite bank. There were jetties and lake houses and a line of trees fringing the shore. If I hit land or a building at this speed, I would either be badly injured or dead. At the last minute, I turned into the wind and came down barely on the shore, in about three or four feet of water. I was pretty shaken up."

When the Zodiac crew came around to pick us up, the sergeant had a whole lot to say about it. Later, I told him what had happened – that I had been ordered by the jump master to turn away from the wind – and I could see by his reaction that he knew just what I was talking about. That order from that major was true toxic leadership. There must be something wrong with that guy's brain wiring for him to order me to execute a maneuver that could have killed me. And it probably could have killed him too. We were not trained to do that. That is toxic leadership right there. That major was not much respected, and certainly not liked by anyone, and although I understand that he probably had some sort of mental issue, he had no business commanding men.

A colleague in that unit told me that that major would follow him around in his car at night, stalking him, trying to find something negative about him during his off-duty hours. I definitely knew to stay away from him, and I did.

Both men – Ellenburg and that major – had a similar outlook and a similar approach, and they both even looked kind of similar. On paper, there was not a whole lot to choose between them. I think maybe if Ellenburg had not been sensitive enough to notice the subtle signs of change in me, things might have been different. After CCF, he could have kept on drilling down on me until I was processed out. Probably then, for the rest of my life, I would have reflected on him in a very negative way. As it happens, I rank him, besides my father, as the most positively influential man in my life.

Years later, when I published my memoir, I sent him a signed copy. By then he was an older man, retired, and living in North Carolina. My cover letter thanked him for his contribution to my life. He read the book, and ordered his entire family, and a bunch of friends, to read it too. Knowing the guy the way I do, I think they probably did what they were told. He wrote me a ten-page letter, talking a little about his career and his methods, and along with that, he sent his drill sergeant's hat as a gift to me. That was a pretty honest and sincere gesture.

As for the other guy, that major who tried to mess with my head and get me killed jumping out of a damn airplane on a water jump, well, he got no signed copy of my memoir.

THE QUESTION THAT I ASKED MYSELF for a long time was what made one of those guys toxic and the other not. Let's take a look at flawed leadership from a few different points of view, and see if we can nail down what a toxic leader looks like.

The word 'toxic' is a fairly broad umbrella term to describe a lot of leadership styles that in one way or another are not productive. In this book, I hope to cover the issue of bad leadership, not only in the military but also in other areas of life and career where fixed hierarchies are in place to manage an organization.

I was fortunate as I was researching this book to have the opportunity to chat with an Army Chaplain. The role of an Army Chaplain is very loosely defined, and in many respects, they can provide an informal ear to listen to complaints and to offer advice and guidance. They also, of course, deal with the spiritual body of the United States Army. They typically have an open door to the commander and can mediate if the situation allows. We will talk a little bit about the role of the Chaplain in a later chapter, but for the moment, when I asked him if he could define toxic leadership, and after thinking for some time, his reply was this:

"Toxic leadership is all kinds of leadership where the leader's actions are ultimately harmful to their followers and the organization, and it is characterized by a lack of concern for the well-being of subordinates. They often use manipulation, usually through fear. They tend to be inwardly focused, self-centered, and driven by self-promotion. They work off the sweat equity of others, and they tend to foster a negative work environment. They are often focused on short-term goals and outcomes without a whole lot of concern for the long-term consequences."

That description was spot on, and I would hear it reflected in the subsequent testimonies of a lot of people I spoke to. A lack of empathy, self-serving, manipulative, and coercive, all with the ultimate aim of self-promotion. The reason that the military is such a breeding ground for toxic leadership, and so a very good template for a discussion of it, is because the system functions on a more rigid hierarchical structure than just about any other organization. As George Reed remarks in his book:

"The military context is different from many others, distinctive and unique for its association with the employment of violence on behalf of the state."[3]

This is surely true. Placing soldiers in harm's way in defense of the nation requires a code of discipline far more stringent and enforceable than anything relevant to an administrative or corporate leadership hierarchy. Soldiers are not typically granted the opportunity to walk off the job in the way that a corporate bureaucrat might, and they certainly do not have unions or trade organizations to negotiate terms of employment. Although mechanisms do exist within the military structure for a soldier to air his or her grievances – the office of the Inspector General is probably the first of those – nothing that quite liberates a soldier from the rigors of military discipline, and the

---

[3] Reed, George E., *Tarnished: Toxic Leadership in the U.S. Military*, Potomac Books. Kindle Edition.

chain of command. It is not, for example, customary in a non-military leadership hierarchy to prosecute a subordinate member for desertion, or failure to obey a lawful order. A corporate employee can just walk off the job if they wish, flipping the bird to the boss on the way out. Try that in the military!

LET'S TAKE A MOMENT TO TRY and get a little deeper into the definition of bad leadership so that a layperson might understand if they are dealing with a toxic or corrosive leader in their chain of command. According to George Reed, leadership across the board can be viewed and assessed on a spectrum.

First of all, a warning! A personality clash, or a passing grievance, does not automatically imply toxic leadership. A demanding leader, or an asshole, is not necessarily a toxic leader. One thing that I have heard time and again in my conversations with junior and senior commanders is that the office of the Inspector General, the much-storied IG, is frequently weaponized, and because of that, individual inspectors often approach a case with healthy skepticism. As George Reed observed, "The intentions of a leader are less important than the perceptions of the followers."[4]

What this suggests to me is that leadership is not just one regrettable incident when a leader is having a

---

[4] *Ibid.*

bad day or a procedural process that a junior ranking soldier does not fully understand, but a pattern of behavior that establishes a negative climate over a long period. There are plenty of examples in history to illustrate this. Probably one of the most famous and celebrated American wartime generals was George S Patton. I enjoy listening to and reading about George S. Patton. Most people remember Patton as the hero of the WWII North Africa and Italian campaigns, one of the great battlefield commanders of our age, but he was also quietly disciplined on the sidelines by General Eisenhower, the Supreme Allied Commander in Europe, for behavior that would get a senior officer relieved in a heartbeat today.

On August 3, 1943, Patton slapped, and verbally abused Private Charles H. Kuhl at an evacuation hospital in Crete, after he was suffering from 'battle fatigue'. A few days later, on August 10, Patton once again slapped a battled-fatigued soldier, Private Paul G. Bennett, and both Bennett and Kuhl were ordered back to the front lines. Patton despised what he perceived as cowardice, and gave orders to his commanders to discipline any soldier making similar complaints.

Eisenhower dealt with the issue when news of the incidents began to circulate back home by quietly pressuring Patton to offer individual apologies to the soldiers concerned, the doctors who had witnessed the episodes, and more generally to the soldiers under his command, through a series of speeches. While

Eisenhower tried to keep a lid on it, the story was eventually picked up by the press, and Patton came under intense public criticism, mainly by Congress, but also by several former generals, including John Pershing. However, as is so often the case, and is one of the great dangers of pursuing a complaint, the military high command, and the Secretary of War, retained Patton as a commander because of his "aggressive, winning leadership in the bitter battles which are to come before final victory."

Clearly, Patton had no empathy whatsoever for soldiers suffering from combat fatigue and Post Traumatic Stress. His behavior was acknowledged and recognized, but the needs of the battlefield of the time kept him from being relieved of his command, although he was denied the opportunity to take part in the mammoth Allied operations on D-Day.

For accusations of toxicity to stick, there needs to be a clear pattern of behavior. One of the most commonly cited examples of this that I heard was "berating and belittling" subordinates in front of their colleagues, and even worse, in front of their subordinates. Lesson one in good leadership is *never* to humiliate or belittle an individual in the presence of others, and if an ass-chewing is demanded, that should be done behind closed doors, and never discussed thereafter. If your commander has a habit of doing that, then you know that you are dealing with a toxic individual.

One time, during chemical training before my attachment to the 10th Special Forces Group, I figured I would put an advertisement in the local camp newspaper for any old examination papers that I could study from. I admit that this was stupid. News of that found its way back to the office and I was given an ass-chewing by my commander. It was done behind closed doors, never spoken about outside of that office, and in the end, he complimented me on great test results. I have always admired that commander.

Micromanaging is another common characteristic of toxic leaders. Micromanaging really kills me, because creativity is how I get around my learning disabilities. The sense that no subordinate is capable of performing any task without the detailed supervision and direction of the leader is a sure sign of toxicity, especially when it is accompanied by the berating and belittling pattern when minor mistakes are made. The stress that this can bring to bear on an individual suffering under it cannot be overstated.

Something that you are likely to hear a lot about in this book is "kiss-up-and-kick-down". George Reed pointed this out to me, and it is referenced in his book. "They tend to be responsive and even obsequious to superiors," He wrote, "while inflicting misery on subordinates. In other words, they tend to kiss up while kicking down. As a result, toxic leaders don't look so bad from the top down while their suffering subordinates wonder how the organization could be so callous as to intentionally inflict such treatment upon them."[5]

Combine this with the fact that senior commanders will often overlook negative patterns of behavior taking place lower down the chain of command if that leader gets results, which, unfortunately, a whole lot of toxic leaders do. This was precisely the situation with General Patton. A signature diagnostic feature of toxic leadership is ambition, drive, and determination. Those characteristics are not in and of themselves toxic, but if those results are achieved on the backs of subordinates, then they definitely are.

What are some other characteristics of a toxic leader?

Well, another word that my friend the Chaplain, and many others besides, mentioned, was *narcissism*. That is the word that has appeared with the greatest regularity in all of the conversations and interviews I have conducted in preparation for this book. Some of the other frequently used terms to describe toxic leadership are *incompetence, malfunction, maladjustment, malcontent, a sense of inadequacy, amorality, cowardice, ambition, egotism, arrogance, deceptive, malevolent* and *malicious*, and many others.

---

[5] Reed, George E.. *Tarnished: Toxic Leadership in the U.S. Military* (Toxic Leadership in the Military) (p. 19). Potomac Books. Kindle Edition.

Let's start with narcissism, the most common. According to the Oxford English Dictionary, the psychopathy of narcissism is defined as *'...selfishness, involving a sense of entitlement, a lack of empathy, and a need for admiration, as characterizing a personality type.'*

I feel that the term 'narcissism' is a bit overused these days, but perhaps it is just that narcissism is more prevalent in the modern world of social media, selfies, and group affirmation. It implies any individual holding themselves in high esteem, or who is conspicuously self-absorbed, which speaks for a lot of people these days. However, such an exaggerated sense of one's own capacity and brilliance can only aggravate underlying tendencies of toxic leadership. The grand-daddy of all narcissistic leaders was Adolf Hitler, but others, like Josef Stalin, Mao, Benito Mussolini, Napoleon, the various North Korean Kims, Saddam Hussein, and Muammar Gaddafi, all conform to this type. Although they inspired dedicated, even fanatical followers, they also all wrought awesome destruction on their nations and societies and left piles of bodies in their wake.

My sense of what makes narcissistic leaders so toxic is a lack of self-reflection. It is almost a cliché these days that a narcissist in charge will claim every team success as their own, and deflect every failure by blaming their subordinates. Narcissism, as a critique of leadership, is also a minefield because, as leadership experts are always reminding us, a certain amount of narcissism is necessary for any individual to generate such sentiments as pride and honor, which are worthy attributes in a soldier.

Narcissism is also essential to self-belief, without which no one can lead. How can a person without confidence and a strong sense of self-worth ever hope to influence other people? Although it is to the ultimate advantage of the organization that the best and brightest within it aspire to, and strive to attain leadership positions, the few who prioritize their interests and objectives above those of the organization can very easily morph into tyrants who will do just about anything to advance those career interests. It leads to a sense of personal exceptionalism or the belief that the normal rules of behavior do not apply to them and that their exalted mission somehow justifies the tyranny that they are guilty of.

"Narcissists are frequently found in positions of power and responsibility because they tend to self-nominate for challenging leadership positions."[6]

Again, narcissism exists on a spectrum, it is not an all-or-nothing phenomenon. Studies show that a little bit of narcissism may be good. Obviously, too much is trouble, and as a general proposition, narcissists are drawn to positions of authority because that

[6] Reed, George E.. *Tarnished: Toxic Leadership in the U.S. Military*. Potomac Books. Kindle Edition.

offers them scope to express their grandiose vision and exaggerated self-image. However, they are often buoyed up in this regard, and conspicuously successful, because they display considerable competence, and very often get the job done. For that, they are appreciated by their superiors, and that remains the case until the destructive qualities of their leadership become inescapable. Such was the case with General Patton. The defense establishment at a critical juncture in the war placed greater value on his competence than the obvious deficiencies of his leadership style. The likely reality is that they will either be promoted or rotated out before their negative attributes start to become a problem for their superiors, even though they have been a problem for their subordinates for their entire assignment.

In summary, a narcissistic leader may tend to be individualistic in outlook, poorly responsive to a free and open exchange of viewpoints and information, and generally best disposed to sycophants and yes-men. Mistakes are seldom owned or acknowledged, advice is routinely ignored, and they are always alert to any opportunity to humble or diminish subordinates. Narcissistic leaders tend to be uncomfortable in situations and climates that require collective capacity, preferring usually to control the agenda, to limit open dialogue, and almost always to restrict the involvement of anyone they perceive as disagreeing with them. What you will hear often from an overtly narcissistic leader is – "There is the right way, the wrong way, the

Army way, and my way. As long as we do things my way, we will get along."

In the face of an attitude like that, any independent thought and decision will likely be rewarded with a gale of invective and belittlement, even if a subordinate follows orders to the letter, according to the demands of his commander. If things go wrong, it will always be someone else's fault, usually a subordinate, and if you are that subordinate, good luck protesting. On the other hand, if the unit experiences conspicuous success, you can be sure that the toxic commander will take all and every credit for it.

Many of these characteristics I can identify in a certain Colonel (retired) Ted Small, a central character in my memoir, and a major player in my own toxic leadership experience. Ted Small was a military technocrat, and a world-renowned researcher, and almost everyone I know agrees that he had the greatest credentials. He was definitely smart, and very skilled in his craft. Ted Small was an entomologist in the academic sense of the word, a researcher and ivory tower academic who also had a species of Korean mosquito named after him. He had married into Korean life, identified entirely with his field, and aggressively defended his claim to prominence in that field. I feel he was very well renowned, not just there in Korea, but all over the world. When he reached mandatory retirement after thirty years, he transferred to the role of a civilian contractor, but remained in the same office, doing the same job, and with the same defensive attitude towards the fiefdom that he had constructed throughout a long career in his field in South Korea.

Then, into the picture came me. I walked in as a good 'ole boy from South Carolina, barely literate, speaking in a southern drawl, and who also claimed to be an entomologist. However, he saw me as a fake entomologist, which may be quite correct, because my job was not about researching the damn mating habits of a mosquito, but making sure that they were eradicated, and that the porta potties were cleaned up and so I looked at myself as mainly a preventive medicine. I looked at my job as leadership. I had no interest in his world of research. I told him that I did not care to publish papers. That was a mistake in hindsight because the research was Ted's baby, and I did not cooperate, and I certainly did not care much for his academic achievements, and that is when the shit began to happen.

Ted Small typifies yet another characteristic common among truly toxic leaders. He identified so completely with the institution that the boundary between his own, personal interests, and the interests of the institution that he served, became blurred. Another characteristic that Ted Small shared with some of the more famous despotic narcissists that we have mentioned was a tendency to purge the field around him of anyone perceived to either be hostile, contrary, or just apathetic. I think, in many ways, that is why he was so determined to rid himself of my presence because he did not perceive me to snap my heels and stand to attention at his request. While I acknowledge his brilliance – and he surely was an academic of the highest caliber – I did not fall in line and clap like a chimpanzee whenever he entered a room. In fact, in subtle, passive-aggressive ways, I told him to fuck off, and he did not like that. He saw my presence and lack of interest in his greatness as a personal threat. He was no longer military, and no longer part of the chain of command, but his identification with the institution was so profound that he just could not separate himself from it. I figured that there was nothing that he could do to me, but that would turn out to be one of the biggest mistakes that I made in my career. To not try and get along with Ted Small was the biggest mistake of my life, and it would live with me for a very long time.

In the *Military Review* article that I mentioned earlier, entitled *Narcissism and Toxic Leaders,* the observation is made in the opening passage:

"One can argue that most, if not all, toxic leaders suffer from being narcissistic. What is a narcissistic and toxic leader? These leaders are selfish and self-serving individuals who crush the morale of subordinates and units. In the best of circumstances, subordinates endure and survive toxic leaders— then the leader or the subordinate moves, changes units, or leaves the military. However, at worst, a toxic leader devastates the *esprit de corps*, discipline, initiative, drive, and willing service of subordinates and the units they comprise."

I have often heard it said that leadership is a partnership between leader and follower, and that is true, in any set of circumstances. In the United States uniformed services, as with any other similar institution, rank is bestowed from above, decided upon, and acted upon, without the consultation of those being led. The criteria for promotion include but are not limited to, academic accomplishment, physical fitness, military training and experience, combat experience, and leadership skills. What is not considered, at least not at the current time, is the opinion of an individual leader expressed by his or her subordinates. The idea of 360-degree assessments is beginning to take root, but it is still not a particularly widely practiced system.

A 360-degree assessment is when people to the left and right of you, below and above, have some degree of input into your evaluation.

I completed one year as a commander in Afghanistan, and what I learned, in coming to understand the Taliban, is that they have a different view of leadership, where leaders are chosen and anointed by the common consent of those to be led. Military leaders are chosen, and given an arbitrary rank that is relevant only for so long as that individual retains the respect and loyalty of his followers. When that respect and loyalty is lost, that leader is disposed of, and another chosen.

This got me to thinking. Yes, indeed, leadership, even in the ranks of an orthodox military formation, is a partnership between leader and follower. An orthodox military officer cannot be ousted in the same way as a Taliban leader could be, by the common consent of the led, but he can be rendered ineffective by the non-cooperation of his subordinates. A chapter of my memoir entitled 'Red Shit' touches a little bit on this issue, and for the sake of this chapter, I'll briefly review the details.

In short, this was the only time in my thirty-one-year career that I saw anything close to a mutiny. During an extensive period of training at Fort Sam Houston in 1995, a small group of junior officers, including myself, spent a period in South Texas studying medically important insects on the land of a local rancher. I held the rank of captain, while most of my colleagues were lieutenants, and we were led by a Major by the name of Whittle. We were a group of preventive medicine officers on an educational exercise, and not an infantry unit in the field, and so the relationship between us all was collegial and friendly.

As I have already noted, in the military, certain professions automatically attract rank. A doctor, for example, normally enters services at the rank of a captain or a major. Those individuals are typically technocrats, not soldiers in the common sense of the word, and as a rule, they are not required to lead in the same way as the commander of a combat battalion. Major Whittle was one of those. He was an academic, and a herpetologist, and his job was to mentor a bunch of preventive medicine officers in their understanding of medical entomology.

I took a shit one day in a cattle enclosure at the ranch in South Texas, expecting it to be obliterated by cattle overnight, but it was not, and instead, the rancher stepped in it the next morning and communicated his displeasure to Major Whittle. Whittle had a keen sense of protocol, and he was embarrassed, so he chewed me out in front of everyone else. As we have already noted, a clear symptom of toxic leadership is any kind of dressing down delivered in the presence of a soldier's comrades or subordinates, and he certainly did that. He was not, however, a toxic leader, just an inept commander, and there is a difference. George Reed remarked to me in conversation that engineers make the worst leaders.

"I don't know anybody worse." He said. "An engineer wants the right side of the formula to equal the left side of the formula, and people just don`t do that."

I had already had my ass chewed out in the Army six ways from Sunday, so it was like water off a duck's back for me, but the other guys did not like it, and they did not seem to like Major Whittle. Thus, they began working to rule and doing everything they could to frustrate and irritate him. I took Major Whittle's side in it, because I liked him, and I felt some sympathy for him. He had no natural gift for leadership and would have, and should have, been more at home in the field, or a lab, or at his desk, maybe studying snakes or insects. To me, that was a clear example of toxic subordinates. They could not mutiny, or relieve him of his command, so they ganged up against him, and he had no real answer to that.

The issue of toxic peers and subordinates is very much a part of the whole equation, and it needs to be given due consideration. George Reed cites a 2014 study by the *Workplace Bullying Institute* that found that, although most bullies tend to be supervisors, around thirty-three percent of the time the abuse comes from peers at the same level of the organization.

"Those who deceive, manipulate, undermine, and place their personal agendas above the welfare of the unit can wreak organizational havoc."[7]

In the end, Major Whittle pretty much gave up, and by common consent, the whole exercise wrapped up early and we went home. The technical results were disappointing. We did not do a good job in the field. Whittle was stung and emotionally bruised, and the whole thing was substandard. Had he maybe had

---

[7] Reed, George E., *Tarnished: Toxic Leadership in the U.S. Military*. Potomac Books. Kindle Edition.

more developed leadership skills, and had the climate been more disciplined, Major Whittle might have been more effective. Maybe if I hadn't taken a shit in the cattle enclosure, and embarrassed the guy in front of our host, none of it would have happened, but I suspect something would have occurred to trigger a mutiny. It was waiting to happen. Toxic peers and subordinates can be a real issue.

Before we wrap up this chapter, I would like to dwell for a moment on the ideas of 'climate', and how that differs from 'culture'.

Climate is a fairly superficial state of being that is easy to control and manipulate. That exercise in South Texas suffered from a climate of disrespect and personal issues between a commander and his subordinates. Major Whittle, with more force of character, and a less petulant and explosive reaction to my indiscretion, could easily have altered the climate and thus created a more acceptable result. Culture, on the other hand, can be defined by established and pervasive conventions developed over a long period. The culture of medical detachments, for example, tends to be collegiate and professional and rarely is discipline an issue. On the other hand, the culture of combat infantry, or special forces, is much more aggressive and gung-ho.

During my military career, I stepped from one culture into another in a way that very few soldiers do. As I have already noted, my first regular assignment was with the 10th Special Forces Group. It was during this assignment that the water jump episode earlier mentioned occurred, and although that major was as toxic as hell, generally, the culture at the time was permissive, with lines of rank and authority blurred somewhat. It was a masculine environment, characterized by mutual respect across the chain of command, where bad leadership would be identified and dealt with reasonably quickly. Men of the enlisted ranks were encouraged to exchange opinions with officers in a frank and open way, and many of the minor rules and conventions of military life were subordinated to the big picture.

No one wearing a green beret can be regarded as a regular infantry grunt because they are not. They are by definition superior soldiers, superior men-at-arms, and superior human beings. The leaders among them tend to acknowledge and respect that fact, and as a consequence, there is an easy rapport across the ranks. Besides that, the whole "belching, farting, and scratching" thing is just the way that men of a certain character behave when they are around one another. It might seem symptomatic of a lax and undisciplined culture, but when the bullets start flying, and the gears begin to spin, it becomes clear very quickly that this is a well-oiled, well-maintained, and superbly functional machine.

My next deployment was to Korea, into the Medical Service Corps, and it was an entirely different culture. Korea, as I have said more than once, is a small command, but also a vitally important one, so it is top-heavy with very senior command figures. Indeed, it is filled with ambitious people and internal politics, with a lot of soft-bodied folk in administrative positions jockeying for prestige and attention. Its culture is more akin to an administrative bureaucracy than a fighting formation, and petty bickering and infighting are rife. As such, it is a topography littered with landmines, and coming in from a special forces environment, I began stepping on those landmines almost immediately.

That was the culture, and as a serving soldier, you will never change the culture. As George Reed pointed out:

"Culture is a powerful force that has a life span longer than the term of most military leaders. In established organizations, there is typically a culture in place before a leader arrives, and one that abides long after that leader departs. Leaders might be able to influence culture, but they do not control it."

George Reed goes into some detail in how to identify, and potentially reform a culture, but that lies well beyond the scope of what I am trying to achieve here. I am speaking to the common soldier or the common worker in a corporate or government bureaucracy. You will not change organizational culture, be it in the military or elsewhere. Culture ebbs and changes by evolution, and the best that you can do is be aware that it exists and learn to work with it. Anyone who has read my memoir will be aware that I fell foul in a major way of the organizational culture of Korea, and things might have been a lot easier if I had adapted more intelligently to that culture instead of trying to be a special forces guy in a room full of preventive health professionals. Just saying.

This, then, is a sketch of what toxic leadership, and toxicity across the ranks, might look like. There are a good many studies out there that list the minutia of identifying toxic leadership in a million different ways, because, as George Reed said, toxic leadership exists on a spectrum. From the benign battalion chaplain to the irascible tyrant, there is every level and stage in between. In the next chapter, we will look at some of the dynamics of toxic leadership.

SOME OF THE DYNAMICS OF
TOXIC LEADERSHIP

*The system of superordination and subordination is
reinforced by both culture and legal code*

George Reed

L ETS KICK OFF THIS CHAPTER WITH an examination of military leadership, as distinct from civilian.
What is it that makes the military hierarchy so unique?
As George Reed remarked, "The military context is
different from many others, distinctive and unique for
its association with the employment of violence on
behalf of the state."

This I believe is a very important point, because, yes
indeed, the military occupies a very unique space
among the instruments of state. But what are some of
the differences and similarities between military and
civilian leadership structures?

Well, just to get started, the two hierarchies are very
different. The military hierarchy is characterized by clear
lines of authority and command, ostensibly premised

on proven achievement and competence. Civilian hierarchies, on the other hand, are much more fluid and flexible, and senior positions can often be predicated on business ownership or stakeholder status. That is not to say that business owners or founders cannot be ousted from the board, just that they achieve their positions through investment and entrepreneurship, and are not usually subject to the scrutiny of any senior command, nor the ethics standards demanded by an organization like the office of the Inspector General.

Risk and decision-making differ too, because military commanders, especially under combat conditions, are expected to make snap decisions in high-stakes, often life-and-death situations, demanding confidence and deliberation under extreme stress. No business or bureaucratic leader is likely to ever be faced with anything like that, and with available time, and the input of consultants and experts, high-stakes decisions in business are more deliberate, and some might argue, easier.

In the area of missions and goals, military objectives are usually specific and non-negotiable, such as capturing a flag, neutralizing a threat, or securing an area. Business missions and objectives, on the other hand, tend to be related to profit, shareholder contentment, and adaptability to changing market conditions.

Training differs too. Military leaders have access to leadership training in terms of managing units, large and small, under conditions of battle or maneuver, demanding precision and predictability. Civilian leaders might attend those boring conferences or symposiums on how to lead a department, but basically, their training will be in their field of expertise, with the leadership aspects of their jobs often incidental. We have discussed culture already, and we know that military culture encourages discipline, loyalty, and sacrifice, while civilian organizations tend to prioritize creativity, diversity, and social responsibility.

And then we have that wonderful animal known as the *bureaucracy*, a strange creature that can ruminate pointlessly for decades, motivated by conformity and dedicated to its perpetuation. Well, perhaps that is not entirely fair, but for the cultivation of organizational inefficiency, predatory politics, and the careful nurturing of dead wood, it's tough to beat a government agency.

Although bureaucratic leadership also functions within a hierarchy, it tends to be more complex and decentralized, and probably way more prone to internal politics and the generation of toxic leadership than any other area of collective human function. Bureaucratic decision-making is about as risk-averse as it is possible to be, especially if the head of that department is an elected official. The process is characterized by committees, consultation, the analysis of data, the input of stakeholders, and a careful effort to remain within ideological parameters, all contained in an environment of wildly diverse levels of red tape and management. No hierarchy in the spectrum of human experiences exemplifies 'culture' quite like an over-blown government bureaucracy, and non-conformity within that culture, which, in many cases, is just ideological dogma, can have very severe ramifications on a person's job or career.

So, while we are mostly emphasizing the military in our examination of toxic leadership, there are probably more people out there dealing with oppressive environments and destructive leadership in the millions of cubicles that make up almost any civilian, bureaucratic department. I hope this book helps in your journey too!

Alright, returning to the military. We started with the observation that the military stands apart because it is armed, and as an organization, it is the iron fist that maintains the sovereignty of the state. Here lies the reason, self-evident for sure, for elevated standards of discipline in the military. A nation's armed forces always hold the potential to interfere with or disrupt the democratic process. Here in the United States, we take for granted the neutrality of the military, and the fact that it resides under the command of a Commander-in-Chief, who is the President. We take that for granted, certainly, but do we always appreciate that it is the enhanced discipline within the uniformed services that sustains that neutrality?

Thus, the military, with its finger on the trigger, cannot be granted the same leeway given to civilian civil servants or corporate functionaries. For the military to hold together and function as the power-projection arm of the state, without periodically turning on the government itself, the individual rights of the soldier must as much as possible be superseded by the well-being of the institution as a whole. In turn, the institution must remain subservient to the state, represented by the President as commander-in-chief, regardless of party. As my friend quoted earlier said, it is not about the individual, but the collective. It is not about the soldier but the platoon, and it is not about the platoon but the company, and so on. Again, for the military to hold that entire edifice in order, the interests of the edifice as a whole must always supersede the interests of the individual soldier. That is why the military is so protective of its command structure, and so often immovable in the face of abuse emanating from within that command structure.

A lot of people I have spoken to, especially those in retirement who have reached positions of leadership, have tried to make the point that strong discipline has to be established from the onset. On the understanding that that individual is at some point destined to find themselves on a battlefield, that disciple must be rigorous and uncompromising. Any kid fresh out of school who has been driven through the gates of an Army basic training facility will have that reality burned into their memory. The standard drill sergeant methodology is intended to be terrifying, and usually it is, but does that make it toxic? Those guys are there to do a job, and that job is to break down the individual and build up the team, and most soldiers will acknowledge once they are through it that it worked. However, that tendency to lead with strength and discipline infuses the entire structure, and can very easily overlap into toxic or corrosive behavior. Give anybody a little power and authority and that amplifies the potential for them to abuse it. It is human nature.

LEADERSHIP ACROSS THE BOARD, both within the military and without, exists on a spectrum. Everyone who is elevated to a position of leadership will find themselves somewhere on that spectrum, ranging from sound, motivating, and inspirational to malignant, corrosive, and toxic. Most advice given on this subject will point to identifying a pattern of behavior rather than an individual waking up with a hangover, missing their morning coffee, and behaving for the rest of the day like an asshole.

During my deployment to Afghanistan, in command of a preventive medicine unit, I was confronted by a situation in which my executive officer, a man by the name of Captain José Vasquez, took to behaving in a very destructive manner toward a team leader serving under him. I will deal in more detail with this issue a bit later, but what made it clear to me that he was a toxic leader, and in my situation, a toxic subordinate, was the consistency of his behavior. It began with a certain amount of surliness and non-cooperation, but it evolved quickly into niggling, baiting behavior, petty criticism, and endless complaints pushed up the chain of command. This went on for about a year, until the first sergeant, who was a woman, appealed to me for some sort of direct intervention. Captain Vasquez was ten years enlisted, and ten years an officer. I counseled and spoke to him endlessly. I felt like I was talking to a rock. He seemed to enjoy the distress he was causing, and if anything, the intervention made it worse. He threatened me with an IG complaint and accused me of racism, and the detachment, as a whole, of animosity against him. It was an impossible situation, and in the end, he was shipped out, a little early, for reasons of health. He definitely had mental issues going on. He was a man eaten up by his own bitterness and disappointment, inclined to lash out and blame everyone around him, and most importantly, he was entirely without empathy.

Empathy is a key aspect of sound leadership, and a lack of empathy is a dead giveaway that you are dealing with a toxic leader. One of the more interesting conversations I had in preparation for writing this book was with an Air Force Pararescue Specialist who served with a tier one special forces unit. These are the best of the best. This is a summarized version of what he told me:

"This particular mission was a mass casualty event. We went in while there was still a heavy firefight underway. We landed, and I think we ended up pulling ten or twelve casualties out of there. The helicopter had been so badly shot up during the operation that it was unflyable by the time we made it back to base. This time I had just really risked my life...this was one of the times when I really thought I was going to die...

"So as we were getting back, I had taken my helmet off, and I sat back there in the helicopter, leaning back, relaxed, and breathing a sigh of relief. I could not believe that I survived that mission and that it was all over. Then our troop commander showed up at the door, and asked, 'Is everybody okay'"

"I said 'Yup.'"

"'What do you need?' He asked.

"Well we need to take everything off this aircraft...we can't fly it, they`re going to send it back...put on the spare aircraft so we can get back up and running...we got to clean it... it's covered in blood..."

"Okay, cool." He replied. "Two things...one thing is the Colonel over there, he told me to tell you guys you need to shave. He saw that a couple of guys weren't freshly shaved, and you need to wear a helmet when you are flying in the helicopter..."

Where was that Colonel's, and that troop commander's empathy? Here was a squad of guys just come in from a heavy action, stabilizing injuries under fire, and evacuating survivors in a helicopter that was taking heavy incoming. Typically those guys operate on rotating twelve-hour shifts, and in a state of exhaustion, stress, and relief, they made it back to base. There some soft-bodied garrison commander had an issue with the fact that some of the men were not freshly shaved!

Unprintable language punctuated that story.

That is an empathy issue. A commander with the best interests of his men at heart would have approached a squad of soldiers freshly home from a grueling combat assignment, stained with the blood of comrades, with nothing but concern for their safety and well-being. Perhaps at a later time, during a less emotional debrief, the issue of shaving might have been raised, but even then, it would likely have seemed petty and trivial in the face of what men were expected to deal with.

Most writers and academics struggle to pin down anything like a universal definition of toxic, or destructive leadership, some just satisfying themselves with the idea that, like good leadership, toxic leadership is something you will know when you see it. One particular scholar on this subject, John P. Steele, makes the sobering point – "Results confirm that leaders who were classified as toxic got their intended results more than any other leadership type."[8]

---

[8] Steele, John P. *Antecedents & Consequences of Toxic Leadership in the U.S. Army: A Two Year Review and Recommended Solutions.*

That tends to confirm an observation that has popped up a few times, that toxic leaders are often mission-driven and ambitious people who achieve excellent results and generally are highly thought of by their superiors, regardless of how poorly regarded they are lower down the chain of command.

My friend, the retired Air Force Pararescue Specialist, related another story to me that defines a couple of characteristics of toxic leadership. The leader in question was, at the time of the incident, a one-star general, and according to his official biography: "He served as the commander of Air Force Special Operations Command from June 2019 to December 2022, having previously served as the vice commander from July 2018 to June 2019 and chief of staff of United States Special Operations Command from June 2017 to June 2018. [He] was commissioned through the ROTC program at Auburn University in 1989. In September 2023, [he] was nominated for promotion to general and appointment as vice chief of staff of the Air Force."

Clearly, an ambitious and upwardly mobile individual.

In October 2019, the Air Force Special Tactics, 14 Special Operations Wing, posted the following announcement: "U.S. Air Force Tech. Sgt. Peter Kraines, 33, a Special Tactics pararescueman with the 24th Special Operations Wing, died from injuries sustained in a training incident while performing mountain rescue techniques in Boise, Idaho."

The back story to this is told by my friend.

"As team leader, I was preparing my guys for an alert cycle, so I took them out on a climbing trip to Black Cliffs, just outside Boise, Idaho. It was part training and part team-building exercise, just a fun trip that would take in some rock climbing and mountain rescue stuff.

"On the second day, one of the guys climbed the cliff and set up an anchor. I did not get eyes on it because I was the last one to get up there, and by the time I did, they had established a rappel line with that anchor adjacent to the climbing line. The first guy got down safely, so in my mind, even though I had not personally seen it, I figured it was sound. We were all from a top-tier unit, so we were all at the same skill level, and I had no reason to question what had been done. Then, the second guy started his rappel, and he got about halfway down when the anchor failed. He fell about thirty feet or so, coming down hard on the rocks below. The other guy, the one who built the anchor, was tied in at the time, and he was pulled off and fell about sixty to seventy feet, impacting the ground below.

"I was still on the rope. In fact, I had just gotten to the top, and I immediately rappelled down and began treatment. We did our best for about twenty-five minutes until the fire department got there, but ultimately he died.

"As soon as I got back to base, I was called in by our group commander to address the accident investigation. That was pretty much where my fate would be decided. In the end, the accident and safety investigation read that there was nothing done wrong. Nothing could have been done differently to change the outcome. The Air Force, however, wanted to hold somebody accountable, and I get that. A guy was killed on my watch, and I was given thirty days to PCS, which for those not in the military, means a Permanent Change of Station. I was being fired, with a Letter of Reprimand, which is almost always the death sentence on any guy's career.

"The guy was killed on my watch, I did not get eyes on the anchor and he had not been wearing a helmet when the incident went down. A helmet likely would not have saved his life, but that was the deal. I was no longer allowed in the building, and I had to clean out my cage on the weekend so nobody else could see. I was leaving a tier one unit to join a regular pararescue squadron. I guess I had it coming.

"The weird shit began when they also fired my commander, and my senior enlisted advisor too. The reason as I see is because they refused to fire me. They said I had done nothing wrong, nothing could have been done differently to change the outcome, and if I am fired the squad will lose trust and become risk averse. Their firing came about because the general, who had recently been promoted, took the time out of his day to reach down to say that this guy – which was me – and his team, *will* be fired.

"Meantime, while this was all grinding through the procedure, I was directed overseas with the largest contingent deployment in the history of the 24th Special Tactics Squadron. Because of the number of aircraft involved, I put in a request for the rest of my group to come out too, so there was a large group of us, the largest group to show up in one area for any contingency operation. That same general officer who fired me took that bullet and used it for his own OPR promotion (OPR is Officer of Primary Responsibility). He took the credit for my operational successes while at the same time firing me. A high five and a stab in the gut at the same time.

[**Author's Note:** what you have right there is a perfect example of a senior officer climbing the ranks on the back of the achievements of his subordinates while withholding credit and recognition to them. Textbook toxic leadership.]

"In the meantime, there was the funeral. We were on an alert cycle, which meant that we could only be a certain amount of time away from the unit, within an hour's radius for phone calls. I scheduled an aircraft to be on standby for the guys on my team to attend the funeral in Arlington, and still remain on alert response. I cleared that with the squadron commander, with the navy, and with the Army, but the group commander denied that for us, and then took that aircraft scheduled for us for himself, so he could go to the funeral and make it back to the fort in time.

"Well, that general officer had no clue the risks that we take, that go with the job that we do. He applied a pilot's mindset to a ground force mission and capabilities. There is a risk that we might lose our lives in training, but that does not mean that because an accident took place, the people involved must be fired. We need to understand what happened and ensure that it does not happen again. That is all. That General Officer is always looking for ways to promote himself, and he is willing to step on the heads of the folks below him to make sure that he looks good.

"Thirty-plus people from the unit dropped in their medical retirement paperwork after that."

I AM NOT A PSYCHOLOGIST, and I do not claim to have any particular insight, but that general officer displayed the classic willingness to climb the ladder on the backs and reputations of his subordinates. My friend offered one example, but a quick internet search throws up a good number of others, so common that is a pattern of behavior.

Another interesting story that emerged during my many conversations with friends was related to me by an active duty reserve major of the United States Army Civil Affairs and Psychological Operations Command. He had a lot of stories to tell, but one in particular that caught my attention involved the "Chunger Games". Again, a brief internet search using those keywords throws up a lot of folk with similar stories. The Chunger

Games were the favorite activity of a senior officer of the SFAB, a certain Colonel Jonathan Chung. My friend served under Colonel Chung when both were with the 10th MTN DIV (LI) Headquarters, in Fort Drum, NY.

The story ran something like this:

"Every month Colonel Chung would do a PT event with all the officers on the staff...we started to nickname them the Chunger Games...he would just smoke us to the point where people were getting injured, and there was only one person left standing. It was always this same dude. He was a special forces major. I swear he was part robot. You just could not smoke that guy."

I did a little research on this guy, Colonel Jonathan Chung, and one of the first things that came up on a Google search was an article in *military.com* under the heading *Commander of Army Pacific Training Brigade Suspended.* The opening paragraph of the article stated simply – "Col. Jonathan Chung was removed this week from his position commanding the 5th Security Force Assistance Brigade after sitting at the helm since July 2021. The circumstances around his suspension are unclear."

'Unclear circumstance' is usually code for some sort of malfeasance. Then I found another article that read *"He Was the Worst Leader I've Ever Had": Suspended Brigade Commander Accused of Toxic Leadership.* That brigade commander was Colonel Jonathan

Chung. Could this be a rare success story, I asked myself, in bringing to account, and removing a toxic leader? I got back in touch with the reserve major and asked him if Chung was a toxic leader.

"Oh absolutely!" he replied. "He was about as toxic as they come."

Colonel Chung, who was a starred West Point graduate, was earmarked for promotion to one star before, in April 2023, he was unexpectedly relieved of his command. Before that, he had been what a lot of guys in uniform describe as a "water-walker", one of those superstars that you run into in the military sometimes. My friend went on:

"He told us that he fought with his first company commander when he was a lieutenant and that he hated that guy. Then he was picked up for below-the-zone promotion to captain, then below-the-zone major and lieutenant colonel.[9] Pretty quickly he lapped his old company commander, who was still a major when he got picked up for lieutenant colonel. He specifically requested for that guy, his old company commander, to be put under his command, just so that he could be an asshole to him, and he made no secret of the fact."

---

[9] BZ (below the zone) means selected for early promotion, a year ahead of primary zone. MB (merit-based) are the first to be promoted from the promotion list and don't have sequence numbers. These folks scored the highest on the promotion board.

A perfect example of "kissing up and kicking down". Just about every book, article, and dissertation on the subject of toxic leadership points to that tendency as a dead giveaway. What it means is that they develop an aspect of diligence, commitment, compliance, and hard work to their superiors, cultivating a positive reputation at the top, while behaving like absolute assholes to those lower down the chain of command. "Kiss up and kick down" is probably the complaint I heard about most in my research for this book.

According to a handful of news sources that covered the story, Colonel Chung was suspended amid allegations of counterproductive and abusive treatment of his subordinates. My friend, the reserve major, ran through a few of his recollections. Colonel Chung, it seems, was guilty of a number of the standard infractions that make enemies out of any soldiers serving under them. He had a well-documented habit of berating men in the presence of fellow soldiers and subordinates, which is another thing that I have heard time and again, and which is also a dead giveaway. He would often compliment his *own* leadership skills, briefly running a podcast covering the subject of leadership, and he leaned on his subordinates to study and comment favorably on each episode. His office wall was heavily decorated with awards and plaques, and again, junior officers and subordinates were pressured to write laudatory comments to be hung alongside. That struck me as yet another common disease of most toxic leaders – narcissism. It is defined by the need to be validated with praise and appreciation, even if most of it was barely hidden sycophancy.

There is no specific background available as to how and under what circumstances the investigation into Colonel Chung was initiated, but according to the reserve major whom I spoke to, enough intelligence was beginning to permeate up the chain of command, and enough guys came together to support an IG complaint, that a full investigation was justified.

Even so, Chung had his supporters. According to *Stars and Stripes:*

"One commander in 5th SFAB said that Chung has an unfair reputation and that his strict leadership style simply rubs some soldiers the wrong way and that they have never witnessed Chung berating or talking down to subordinates."

That is a common enough defense, and I am sure sometimes it is true. Colonel Chung amassed 213 letters of support, including forty-seven members of the 5th SFAB, ranging from enlisted soldiers to general officers. So he certainly had support, but it was obviously not enough. In June 2023, after the investigation, Colonel Chung was formally relieved, and a statement issued by the chain of command stating simply that he had lost the confidence of his command, based on the results of an Army Regulation 15-6 investigation. It does not appear that Colonel Chung received any official sanction or formal reprimand, but was just reassigned, but he did not make one star. To wrap this story up, here is a quote from *Task & Purpose*:

"We got to a point where we just realized that we are in a game that we were designed to lose, the soldier said. If I had to go work for that man again, I'd leave the Army. I would refuse to go work for him – refuse."

So, in a nutshell, how do you know if you are serving under a toxic leader? Well, as George Reed told me, it is impossible to define in clinical terms what makes a toxic leader, and how to identify a toxic leader when you are serving under one, but you will know it when you see it.

MACHIAVELLIAN MARY: WOMEN AND TOXIC LEADERSHIP

'Queen bee' is a derogatory term applied to women who have achieved success in traditionally male-dominated fields. These women often take on "masculine" traits and distance themselves from other women in the workplace in order to succeed. They may also view or treat subordinates more critically if they are female, and refuse to help other women rise up the ranks as a form of self-preservation.

Wikipedia

A CCORDING TO THE DEPARTMENT OF DEFENSE, in 2021, women made up just over seventeen percent of the active-duty force, totaling 231,741 members. While that is an impressive statistic, it still represents just a small percentage, under a quarter, of serving personnel. I served mainly in the medical branches of the United States Army, which put me in contact with a lot of women, and besides one or two difficulties, which had more to do with me than them,

I only had one single episode of toxic leadership at the hands of a woman, and man it was a doozy.

I thought a lot about doing this chapter, and I understand that it is probably going to be less than politically correct. I got to thinking about it mainly because a good number of men that I spoke to, who opened up about their experience at the hands of a toxic leader, referred to 'her', and 'she', as they told their stories, and I wondered what that could mean in the big picture. I began searching around for some reference or documentation on the subject, and what I found was a master's thesis entitled *Females and Toxic Leadership*, attributed to the corporate authorship of the Army Command and General Staff College, Fort Leavenworth KS. This document posed the simple question *"Is there a gender component in toxic leadership?"*

It is a fair question, but I would guess likely impossible to truthfully answer in the social environment of the moment. What was revealed in this document is that women suffer disproportionately from toxic leadership in the ranks of the military, *simply because they are women*. That is very safe ground, and it is probably self-evident. A trickier avenue of inquiry would be, how do women contribute to toxic leadership, and how susceptible are they to destructive behavior at a command level?

Let's deal with the first thing first. In a traditionally male environment, particularly in the combat branches of the military, there will inevitably be a period of institutional adjustment as more and more women appear in uniform. That just reflects our wider society, and there is no real surprise there. The environment of Korea, under the leadership of Colonel Martha Stewart, who is a central character in my own story of toxic leadership, was pretty sexist, and the explanation for why she was so damned difficult was that she was gay, she was menopausal, or she was frustrated, and it went on all the time. It was not difficult to detect, because she overtly had some mental health issue, probably having to do with anger, and I am sure that she knew what was being said about her.

So, even in that situation, the worst toxic leader I have ever experienced, who was a woman, was also on the receiving end of some very toxic, sexist behavior. As an old cynic, however, all I saw in *Females and Toxic Leadership* was an expression of victimology without any real effort to add any substance to the question, can women in command be susceptible to toxic behavior to a greater or lesser extent than men?

Colonel Martha Stewart became the stuff of nightmares to me. She was tight with Colonel Ted Small, the guy that I earlier described, and the contractor, and he used her to get at me. I'll touch on the details of that a little later in this narrative, but how her behavior stood out as toxic was pretty damn classic. She had a distinctly bipolar personality. Some days she would walk into the office with home-baked goodies to hand out to her staff, all sweet and kind and light, and everybody who had any sense of self-preservation at all would savor them, I know I did, and say, "Hey these are great! How`d you do it!"

More commonly, she would come in brooding under a dark cloud, moody and volatile, itching for a confrontation, and unconcerned who in particular came under her wrath. Her responses were way out of proportion to any offense that caught her attention, and often it was clear to everyone that she was venting some inner fury that reflected nothing that we had done, or could do. She had no filter, no ability to moderate the insulting and demeaning tone of her language, and usually, when it was over, she would retreat to her office, slam her door, and brood silently for hours. I only had to deal with her for a few months, because she shipped out to Hawaii, on April 30, 2008, a date I will never forget. Those few months were the most scarring of my entire experience in uniform.

Indeed, women certainly are victims, anyone at the receiving end of toxic leadership *is* a victim, but can women also be perpetrators? As I began to talk to people and dig more deeply into the issue, I discovered, as with everything, that the situation is a lot more nuanced and complicated than the current doctrine would suggest.

The main contributor to this chapter is a retired senior officer of the Army Medical Services, Colonel Jennifer

Caci. Colonel Caci's mantra throughout our interviews was her belief that the male-dominated command structure in the US military cannot, as a body, cope with strong, willful, and competent women, and many formal studies back this up. She also made the point that as women begin to proliferate in greater numbers throughout the uniformed services, and routinely arrive at positions of command, the day is fast approaching when powerful women will no longer be the exception, but a standard feature of military life. When that happens, things might improve.

Colonel Caci commanded the 47th Combat Support Hospital, out of Fort Lewis, Washington, a technical position that required significant experience, expertise, and ability, but also political savvy and a capacity to navigate a challenging chain of command. She described to me several assignments and circumstances where she found herself under toxic male command. One story in particular that caught my attention related to a field exercise planned for the 47th Combat Support Hospital, to be held at Joint Base Lewis McChord in Washington, in October.

A Combat Support Hospital is a mobile field hospital typically established in an area of operations to deal with battlefield casualties. Command of, and deployment with, a CSH is a highly technical and detailed business, requiring much coordination and a great deal of training and planning. Training operations are vital to the smooth function of a CSH, and putting such an exercise together is not something that can be achieved overnight. I have never done this work but I know it takes a lot of organization. The exercise was eight months in the planning, and it was scheduled for October because that is typically a dry month in the Pacific Northwest.

This is where it gets kind of crazy. Late in August, orders came down through the chain of command informing Colonel Caci that the commanding officer, her boss, wanted to schedule a maintenance shutdown for October and that her exercise was to be delayed for a month.

Apart from the inconvenience of having to reschedule a complex operation at the last minute, November in Washinton State is likely to be wet, a detail that would heap complications on the operation. Even if it were not wet, the delay was a significant complication. It would probably be fair to say that the commander was aware of this detail, and was trying to set Colonel Caci up for failure. That is a pretty standard tactic of toxic leaders.

"......the guy hated me," Colonel Caci told me. "He hated me partly because I knew more than he did, but also because I was a woman, I was single, I didn't have children, I didn't go to church on Sunday, so I did not fit any of the criteria that he thought officers should."

No amount of persuasion and compromise would change the commander's mind, and the exercise went ahead in November, and despite difficult conditions, it was a success.

"We learned a lot of good lessons...but he did it on purpose, because the unit was successful, and he did not like that, he didn't want the 47th Combat Support Hospital to succeed, and we did, and he hated that. Instead of embracing it and saying 'Hey look at this great unit that I have', he thought that if he made me move that field problem forward a month we would fail. Well, we did not."

As I reflect on Colonel Caci's situation, I can see that she was almost tricked into failure. I was also tricked into failure, but I did not handle it as well as she did. She came out of it successfully.

Of the four men whom Colonel Caci worked for during the second part of her career, all were physicians – the first an oncologist, and the others family doctors. That aligned, in my mind, with George Reed's observation that engineers make the worst leaders. Physicians, like engineers, are technocrats, and as serving officers, they are administrators running some medical division or another. They are not combat soldiers, and so they are not held to the same standard of leadership as the commander of a combat unit.

"I have worked for many very good physicians." Colonel Caci went on. "And although the majority of them might have been good doctors and fair-minded human beings, they were atrocious leaders. I learned entirely too much about narcissistic personality disorder because of these people I worked for."

This led our discussion back down that rabbit hole that quite a few conversations have already followed. *Narcissism!*

Narcissism is an easy word to toss about, and a lot of people use it liberally without really having any clinical sense of what it implies. Colonel Caci, however, knows precisely what she is talking about, and she continued:

"So here's what I think: typically they are very driven. They are characteristically very successful, and very intelligent, and they completely lack empathy and sympathy. But they are effective, and when you look at them on paper, they look pretty good."

The theme of Colonel Caci's experience as a high-ranking officer is that her mere presence was disconcerting to senior, male commanders. My conversations with her left me in no doubt that she is a woman of great confidence and capacity, highly trained and widely experienced, whose technical and administrative functions she was more than capable of handling. Part of that is probably inherent, but a lot of it has been acquired through hard work, diligence, and a clear sense of mission. It does not surprise me that she found herself up against male superiors who were intimidated, and to assert themselves, were likely more than a little obstructive and condescending.

"The last time I sat down with him." She recalled, of a particularly difficult officer. "I looked at him and I said 'What is it about me that you have such a problem with? What have I done over these two years?' And you know what he did? He raised his hands into the air, and he looked at me and said, 'It's just everything!' What do you do with that?"

During this same conversation, a term was used once or twice that caught my attention: *'Moral injury!'*

After a little bit of research, I understood that moral injury is a psychological term closely allied in the military context with PTSD and depression. I found numerous definitions, but the most succinct is lifted from the *Disabled American Veterans* website, stating: "Moral injury is when one feels they have violated their conscience or moral compass when they take part in, witness or fail to prevent an act that disobeys their own moral values or personal principles."

Looking back at my own PTSD, I concluded that a lot of it had to do with toxic leadership, and a lot of it was also associated with moral injury. I feel that.

The concept of PTSD in the military is generally understood to relate to combat-associated stress and trauma, but actually, there is more to it than that. My most profound experience of toxic leadership was during that third deployment to Korea. Third Time a Charm I called it in my memoir. That situation was a turf war in the small kingdom of entomology and preventive medicine in the 18th MEDCOM, and the tactic employed against me was to drop a turd on my plate and let the smell of it drift up the chain of command. I was accused of pedophilia, in particular interfering with my daughter, and espionage against the United States Government through the many friendly relationships I had with Korean nationals. I went from a pedophile to a spy within one year. Both were vague accusations, their source obscure and unprovable, but potentially serious enough to screw up my world. I felt that I came out of that with severe PTSD, but perhaps more accurately, what it inflicted on me was *moral injury*.

We do not need to get too deeply into the psychology of moral injury here, but I have a feeling that a lot of people out there will know exactly what I mean. The term began to separate itself from the direct experiences of combat when similar symptoms to PTSD began to appear among drone pilots who went nowhere near the combat zone. These individuals engaged directly in operations, and were morally damaged by missions that did not compromise their safety, but did challenge their moral compass.[10] That is somewhat the same as

---

[10] According to **Michael D. Matthews** Ph.D., professor of engineering psychology at the United States Military Academy: *"I suggested that*

serving under, and suffering under, a leader whose behavior is toxic and destructive, in particular if one becomes the subject of that leader's particular attention. There are so many compromises, so much turning of a blind eye, and so much moral injury that the damage can often be permanent.

"These cases do not result from direct exposure to traumatic events, *per se*, but are related instead to violations of moral standards and beliefs, with an attendant and pervasive sense of powerlessness and hopelessness, factors that have long been known to be related to depression and other pathologies."[11]

Yet another arena where the term *moral injury* crops up is in law enforcement, where individuals can often sense that they are working within a hostile and politicized environment, where the chain of command does *not* have their back, and where they are routinely sacrificed to save the careers of superiors. More than that, they consistently find themselves on the frontline, and at daily risk of being sacrificed on the altar of political vengeance and expedience.

---

moral injury is more associated with an existential crisis, stemming from the violation of values pertaining to the sanctity of life, than with trauma. Moral injury, from this perspective, involves a more abstract cause than PTSD, which is thought to occur after direct contact with a traumatic event. The infantry soldier directly sees the impact of his or her actions, available through all of the sense organs. The UAV pilot knows their actions have caused loss of life, but the nexus between their own actions and consequences are less direct."

[11] Michael D. Matthews Ph.D. Psychology Today. *Moral Injury: How organizations and leaders may contribute to or protect against moral injury.* March 10, 2018

An individual like Colonel Caci, as a woman in uniform in the US Army, was constantly confronted with the dilemma of balancing her professional obligations with the political necessities of dealing with difficult, and at times abusive leaders. Another question that I put to her was, how susceptible are women themselves to toxic leadership?

WE ARE LIKELY TO STRAY NOW into territory that is not very politically correct, but it is important to go there. I had many conversations with many people in preparation for writing this book, and as I have already noted, several men who discussed their toxic leadership experiences referred to the offending leader as 'she.' I put it to Colonel Caci that women might have a particular susceptibility to toxic leadership, and she replied that women in command positions, particularly if they are in command of men, find themselves in a situation where they have to be *more*. More driven, more ruthless, more uncompromising, and more mission-orientated, just to avoid the stereotypes, and to be taken seriously. That this can fairly easily overlap with toxic behaviors, or at least behaviors that seem to be toxic, stands to reason. This is just one of the unique pressures that women experience at the highest levels of leadership.

I had the opportunity to chat with a woman, this time a Marine, who had trained under the 4th Recruit Training Battalion at Marine Corps Recruit Depot Parris Island,

South Carolina. The officer commanding that Battalion was Lt. Col. Kate Germano, who was relieved of her command at the end of June 2015, having been found to be "hostile, unprofessional and abusive". I was asked not to publish any verbatim quotes from the conversation, so I will not, but I did dig deeper into the issue, and I was surprised to discover that the affair has been well covered in the press. The full command investigation is, in fact, available in the public domain, albeit heavily redacted, and that made fascinating reading indeed.

The document is almost three hundred pages long and is a very interesting insight into how an investigation of this nature takes place. What is particularly interesting is that the inquiry was triggered by an anonymous whistleblower report, something that usually goes nowhere at all. What it tells me is that enough intel had begun to make its way up the chain of command that even an anonymous complaint had enough credibility about it to motivate the chain of command to act. Attached to the investigation report were a few comments by the Commanding General, Brig. Gen. Terry Williams, that runs as follows:

> Specifically, I concur with the investigating officer's opinion that [Lt. Col. Kate Germano] created a hostile, repressive, and unprofessional command climate that was pervasive throughout her command. The investigation revealed that [Lt.

Col. Kate Germano], on numerous occasions, was abusive towards officers, staff, non-commissioned officers, and junior Marines under her command. She publicly berated officers and enlisted Marines in front of subordinates and undermined the credibility of drill instructors in front of recruits. Furthermore, by...outwards displays of contempt and disgust towards individuals she had conflicts with or who did not perform up to her concept of acceptable standards, [Lt. Col. Kate Germano] created an environment where numerous Marines expressed fear of reprisal for providing statements to the Investigating Officer. Her toxic leadership is wholly unacceptable and not consistent with our core values and leadership principles.

That statement certainly takes no prisoners, and as one reads through the report, it is backed up by numerous sworn statements by individuals who served under her command.

In her defense, Lt. Col. Kate Germano claimed that she was only trying to make the unit better by holding women to tougher standards. The story was picked up and reported by the *Marine Times* of July 2015, and what follows is an excerpt:

"Lt. Col. Kate Germano, the former commanding officer of 4th Recruit Training Battalion at Marine Corps Recruit

Depot Parris Island, South Carolina, was found to be 'hostile, unprofessional and abusive,' according to a command investigation obtained by Marine Corps Times. She was relieved for cause on June 30 by Brig. Gen. Terry Williams, Parris Island's commanding general.

"*But officers who served with her* [author's italics] say she was a blunt reformer who spearheaded efforts to improve recruit training regardless of gender, and that a vocal minority in the battalion undercut her achievements. Germano's tactics, for example, dramatically improved range qualification rates for female recruits.

"The ensuing controversy, some say, provides a glimpse into an ongoing struggle to establish equal standards for male and female Marines at the Corps' East Coast recruit depot. Now Germano is petitioning lawmakers for redress, saying she was treated unjustly by base leadership. Germano declined to provide additional details about those efforts, due to concerns about protected communications to Congress."[12]

The case became a *cause celeb* for advocates against gender bias in the military, and Kate Germano later wrote an influential book, *Fight Like a Girl*, that has become something of a case study for the trials and difficulties confronting women in uniform. Some might say that it was inevitable that Lt. Col. Kate

---

[12] *Controversy surrounds firing of Marines' female recruit battalion CO.* Marine Corps Times, July 7 2015

Germano would claim gender bias in the actions taken against her, although it should be added that she commanded an all-female training battalion, and a majority of those that leveled complaints against her were also female. She later adopted the role of advocate against gender bias in the military and has created a role for herself defending women who have been singled out and punished in the manner that she was.

Another high-profile case was that of Command Sergeant Major Teresa King who, in 2009, gained national attention for becoming the first woman appointed to serve as commandant of the Army's drill sergeant school at Fort Jackson. This case is quite complicated, and I would encourage readers to research it in more detail, but the nuts and bolts of it are this: three years after her appointment, CSM King was fired for creating and perpetuating a toxic work environment. The accusations were general, and probably there was some substance to them, and CSM King was duly held to account and relieved of her command.

She too took the matter further, claiming that sexism and racism (she is an African American woman) were behind the accusations and that she was the victim of a deeper conspiracy to oust her. She was clearly a no-bullshit drill sergeant – "Sergeant Major No-Slack", as she was known – but the question of whether she was actually a toxic leader in the established sense has tended to be obscured by the subsequent dust storm over allegations of racism. Ultimately, she was reinstated, a negative report removed from her record, and through a suit of defamation, some money changed hands.

The very forthright, aggressive, and can-do attitudes of these women ensured that neither they nor quite a few others like them, took matters lying down. It might be said, therefore, that taking down a female toxic leader is a lot more difficult than taking down a man, since women, in particular non-white women, have excellent grounds for appeal built into their circumstances. Nonetheless, the residual conclusion must be that female toxic leaders seem to have the common characteristic that they are strong personalities driven by internal biases to be *more*, much more, just to be taken seriously.

Again, the Lt. Col. Kate Germano case is an interesting one for *another* reason, that her subordinates were mostly women. One of the accusations leveled against her, as contained in her investigation report, was that she "...reinforced gender bias and stereotypes in the minds of the recruits she was entrusted to empower." According to the report:

"During the last two end-of-cycle briefs for graduating Marines, [Lt. Col. Kate Germano] told Marines that male Marines 'would never take orders from them' and the male Marines would always see female Marines as 'weak and less of a Marine' because female Marines are not held to the male physical standards."

AS A MEDICAL OFFICER, I came into contact with a lot of nurses, and there was a saying in the medical services at the time that "Nurses eat their own". I spoke to a leadership expert on this subject, and he directed me to a study of the 'queen bee syndrome', which I thought was probably a minefield, but I stepped in anyway.

A famous encyclopedia, with all of the careful disclaimers one might expect, describes the 'queen bee syndrome' as: "...a derogatory term applied to women who have achieved success in traditionally male-dominated fields. These women often take on 'masculine' traits and distance themselves from other women in the workplace to succeed. They may also view or treat subordinates more critically if they are female, and refuse to help other women rise through the ranks as a form of self-preservation."

The piece then goes on to articulate, in scholarly language, a tendency among women *not* to nurture and mentor the professional development of other, subordinate women, and to be chilly towards other women sharing a platform of success in a male-dominated environment. Although, so potentially awkward would be any discussion of this subject be that most material out there is anecdotal. What it does suggest, though, is that women are not immune to the symptoms of corrosive leadership, and might, because of the particular difficulties and challenges that they face, have a greater tendency to lapse into toxic behavior.

Another term I encountered, as I tunneled a little more deeply into that rabbit hole, was "Machiavellian Mary", which I thought looked and smelled like a legitimate landmine. The journal *Psychology Today* described "Machiavellian Mary" as an extremely derogatory term, intended to imply: "...women who are hostile to nurturance and cooperation, opting instead for aggression and backstabbing to get ahead"[13]

Since I am neither a psychologist nor am I a psychiatrist, and since what I read from the above is just garden-variety toxic leadership, I think the inference we can draw is that toxic leaders can just as easily be women as men, and men suffering under the predations of a female toxic leader can find it as distressing and paralyzing as women trying to function under a male toxic leader, and any variation in between.

Can one, with any scientific certainty, claim that women are more frequently toxic in leadership positions than men, or that they reserve a particular toxicity for other women? Probably not. That is a question for women to answer, according to their own experience, and for

---

[13] Shoba Sreenivasan, Ph.D., and Linda E. Weinberger, Ph.D. *Toxic Femininity: Machiavellian Mary in the Workplace.* November 29, 2017

people more qualified than me to analyze. What is undeniable is that women in uniform, and women in the corporate world, suffer disproportionate attention when it comes to toxic leadership, and even more so sexual harassment, as a factor of toxic leadership.

ACCORDING TO GEORGE REED, and I agree: "Sexual misconduct is a behavior that is not only corrosive to good order and discipline in military organizations, it also constitutes an overwhelming breach of faith, especially when it involves subordinates."

No truer word was ever spoken, and here again, I will refer to Lt. Col. Kate Germano's investigation report:

"[Lt. Col. Kate Germano's] position on sexual assault is inconsistent with the clear standards provided in...regulations. Although she is permitted to have personal opinions that are different from those of the institution, her messaging that sexual assault is '100% preventable' and those who drink and put themselves 'in a position to be sexually assaulted' fostered a climate where some members of her command felt she blamed the victim and, accordingly, they would not feel comfortable reporting a sexual assault."

What that tells me is that the issue of sexual assault in the military, and elsewhere, is probably the most difficult of toxic behaviors to deal with. It is a facet of that behavior that can have the worst ramifications, and impose arguably the greatest moral injury. An excellent leader can achieve the right balance between detachment and empathy, to appear composed and competent, while also accessible and human. Unwanted sexual pressure or overtures within the chain of command, in particular, if it involves a subordinate, epitomizes toxic leadership. That is because it implies a lack of concern for the welfare of a subordinate as well as compromising the distance that is essential for a good professional relationship.

Here are a few technicalities regarding fraternization in uniform. The Uniform Code of Military Justice is somewhat vague in its detailing of what fraternization represents, and how to deal with it. Nonetheless, the issue is dealt with in Article 134, the opening preamble which states:

"In general, the gist of this offense is a violation of the custom of the armed forces against fraternization. Not all contact or association between officers and enlisted persons is an offense. Whether the contact or association in question is an offense depends on the surrounding circumstances. Factors to be considered include whether the conduct has compromised the chain of command, resulted in the appearance of partiality, or otherwise undermined good order, discipline, authority, or morale. The acts and circumstances must be such as to lead a reasonable person experienced in the problems of military leadership to conclude that the good order and discipline of the armed forces have been prejudiced by their tendency to compromise the respect of enlisted persons for the professionalism, integrity, and obligations of an officer."

I have experience in my past of breaking this fraternization regulation. As a young officer in the National Guard, I was involved in a brief relationship with a junior colleague, which caught the attention of my CO. I was called in and asked to sign a cease and desist letter regarding this relationship. My CO was very angry, and because of it, my evaluation was hosed. As I understood it, only fraternization *within* the chain of command was against regulations, but in fact, the regulations are more general than this. They read (Army Regulation (AR) 600-20):

"Certain types of personal relationships between officers and enlisted personnel are prohibited. Prohibited relationships include dating, shared living accommodations other than those directed by operational requirements, and intimate or sexual relationships between officers and enlisted personnel."

Either way, I had a "fuck-you" attitude in those days, and while I signed the document stating that I understood its contents, the relationship went on. It was the Guard, and not the regular Army, so things were a bit more relaxed, and the relationship was wholly consensual, but it was unprofessional nonetheless. I understand that now. It was not sexual harassment, but it had the potential to be portrayed that way, and I cannot say what the woman involved might have felt about that.

The story was kind of dramatic because she was one of very few females in the National Guard at that time. Keep in mind she was also one of the best-looking girls in the unit, so observations and perceptions were focused very much on her regardless of where I stood in the picture.

The bottom line is that the military frowns upon and discourages any kind of intimate relationship across the ranks, but to enforce that would probably be impossible. Considering how many happily married couples met in the military, conducted their relationship, and married while in uniform, it would probably be impossible to do so. The reason behind that is not the one or two who go on to have happy life partnerships, but the tendency of a few to turn bad, to compromise the chain of command, and to end in sexual assault.

When that attention is unwanted, and when the perpetrator is a superior officer, there is almost inevitably an ugly overtone. The phenomenon is also not confined to women. There have certainly been disciplinary actions against senior female officers in their behavior towards men, and towards other women, just as men might find themselves the object of interest of a senior commander who also happens to be a man. It is a tricky state of affairs, and one that senior officers might be forgiven for ignoring, after which the victims simply dust themselves down, compartmentalize their moral injury, and get on with their careers. Even sometimes when passive interest morphs into aggressive interest, and possibly rape, there is a strong incentive to avoid the rigors of prosecution and to just move on.

Keep in mind that the military is a transitional organization, so if you just suck it up, either the subordinate or the senior officer is likely to just move on.

Since October 2012, according to the *Washington Post*, thirty U.S. generals and admirals have been investigated for personal misconduct, seven cases of which involved 'inappropriate' relationships. Probably the most high profile of these was the case of Brigadier General Jeffery Sinclair, who was investigated for a long-standing relationship with a female captain. Initially, both parties agreed that the relationship was consensual, but the impression was left that the female captain was pressured into that admission. When accusations of sexual assault were leveled, Brigadier General Sinclair mounted a "vigorous' defense", and in the end, dodged the bullet that may well have put him behind bars for life. Ultimately, he was discharged at a rank two grades lower than his one star, leaving the military after twenty-eight years at the rank of Lt. Col.

As an interesting side note, I had the opportunity to chat with a female medical officer who made a few points worth including here. One was that she joined the military a lot later than most – she was thirty when she signed up – so she was protected a little bit by age and maturity, but she added that sexual assault was, and still is, rampant within the services. She also told me the story of a young female enlisted private who was raped by her sergeant. The situation was cut and dried and was taken seriously, but she was reassigned and placed elsewhere to await the result of the investigation, while the perpetrator was not. Within that lies the classic lack of empathy for the victim that so characterizes toxic leadership. Ultimately, justice was done, insofar as the guilty member was tried and punished appropriately, but the slight delivered on the victim by her having to relocate irritated a lot of women in the ranks.

As many who I chatted to in preparing this chapter reminded me, victims of sexual assault are not exclusively women, and that a surprising number of men also find themselves at the receiving end of unwanted sexual attention. An interesting story was told to me by a military chaplain regarding a consultation between him and a young, married private. The private's sergeant took an interest in the wife of his subordinate, and would regularly visit his on-base home, enter uninvited and effectively rape his wife. The Chaplain, when told this story, was astonished, and asked why the hell the young man did not just throw the sergeant out.

"Can I do that?" He asked.

"Yes, you can do that!" The Chaplain replied. "And you can kick his damn ass too!"

Sexual misconduct will be an inevitable corollary of increased female enrollment, but it must be understood that such misconduct is toxic in the truest sense of the word, and likely the most damaging behavior across the spectrum. It is also one of the most difficult to prove, litigate, and gain reasonable redress from, and even with such redress, the 'moral injury' inflicted will remain. The advice that I was given by several women who offered input for this book is not to feel intimidated by the difficulties implied by confronting sexual harassment or sexual misconduct of any sort. Any reading of Army regulations and guidelines will convince you that the military takes this issue very seriously indeed, and even though you might be coming up against some heavyweight resistance, David does regularly slay Goliath on this particular battlefield.

In conclusion, a groundbreaking, and award-winning documentary entitled *The Invisible War* was produced in 2012 that exposed sexual assault in the military in greater depth than ever before, and I would urge all those reading this chapter to take the time to watch it. It is available on numerous social platforms. It deals with some of the most extreme examples of sexual violence, mainly against women, in the uniformed services, and highlights numerous examples of women unevenly treated in favor of men under conditions of great stress and moral injury. It would certainly be constructive for anyone wishing to gain some sense of the scope of the problem.

How to Survive and Recover

You will never change someone's behavior. What you can change is how you deal with it.

Ed Evans

O NE DAY, DURING MY THIRD ASSIGNMENT TO Korea, I ran into the toxic leadership scenario from hell. This was probably the worst episode of my entire life. We have touched on it a few times in this book already, but in essence, I was called into the office of my commanding officer, ostensibly to discuss my evaluation report, and told that there was talk about a problem that I had with young children, and in particular my daughter. What I was being told was that I was suspected of being a pedophile, and even worse than that, that I was interfering with my daughter.

That situation almost drove me into a rage. It had been on the boil for some time, but it came to a head on that day. The pretext was a counseling session related to my Officer Evaluation Report, and naturally, the accusations were non-specific, but wicked enough to capture general attention, and sadly, people are often easily persuaded to believe the most outlandish rumors. It happened one day when I was invited into the office of Colonel Martha Stewart for a counseling session related to that upcoming officer evaluation.

The question was put to me how should it be explained on the report that I had a problem with children? Rumors, she told me, were circulating that I had pedophilic tendencies, and what is more, that I was abusing my daughter. I like kids, and I have always got on well with them, and at the time I was spending time at the middle school as part of the reading program, and I was coaching soccer. The rumor was put out there, and from some informal source, kept on the boil. Every day I had to step out of my front door in the closed environment of a military base and go to work, knowing what people were hearing about me, and what many people thought about me. One time I recall, during a charity run on base, that a couple of kids were having trouble with their bikes, and I walked over to help. A fellow officer came hurrying over and said – "Hey, get the fuck away from my kids!"

Colonel Stewart threatened me with a board of inquiry, used mostly to out the soldier in question. What do you say to that? How do you react? I was completely blindsided. I walked away, humiliated, angry, and confused. Alternately I wanted to kill someone, to kill myself, to walk off base then and there, to resign, to scream, or to check myself into a hospital. Later on,

I checked myself into a hospital because I had an anxiety attack. Nothing ever came of it, of course, and no specific evidence was ever presented, nor any detailed accusations of any sort put forward, just the rumor and innuendo, stirred up behind the scenes, and kept on the boil.

It was mostly because of that issue that I set about writing this book. I knew who was behind the rumors, and I knew why. One time my dad and I put together a plan to ambush the individual concerned while we were at a board meeting, and deliver up a beating that he would never forget. In the end, we did not, and I am glad because all that would have achieved would have been to get me charged with assault and locked up, and if he was able to screw up my life so bad with fabricated information, how bad could it be if I gave him grounds?

In the end, thanks to the support of my family, I got through it. Before long my supervisor was reassigned, and I changed units, and the dust began to settle. One of the realities of military life is that an individual serviceman is likely to be reassigned, or rotated out eventually, so often just biting the bullet and taking the shit is the best way to deal with a toxic situation, because either you or that toxic leader is likely to be reassigned in a couple of years, and you can move on to fresh fields. That is the practical advice that a lot of people will offer you if you find yourself dealing with a toxic personality in your chain of command, but let us consider a few alternative options.

First of all, if you are dealing with toxic leadership, take notes! I have a personal philosophy that has served me well throughout my career. In the old days, there was a saying that you would hear a lot when you were around soldiers. I heard it first when I was sitting on my bed in the barracks at Fort Sill, while I was under basic training, field stripping my M-16 over and over again to try and get the knack of doing it. One of the other guys said – "Pike is maxing the Five Ps."

The Five Ps are 'Pre-planning Prevents Piss Poor Performance', and as a philosophy, it applies to just about every aspect of life. In this case, the Five Ps demand that you keep notes, and document every aspect of your experience, bringing on board as many others as possible who are willing to give sworn testimony. Go the extra mile, and cover all of your bases. It will make all the difference when the rubber hits the road.

In the case of Col. Jonathan Chung and Lt. Col. Kate Germano, the complaints against them were backed up by a significant body of documentation and witness statements, enough to overcome the accumulation of positive reviews and reports that both individuals were able to accrue to answer to the allegations. Again, make sure, if you are leading the complaint, that your witness testimony is backed up by written statements. You may be sitting around in the barracks bitching about sergeant this or lieutenant that, and everyone says, "Yeah man, I'm with you brother!", but when shit gets real they back down, and will not commit. Get it all in writing, and if necessary get help to do it. A good place to start is the Battalion Chaplain, who is usually an educated person and is bound to confidentially, so no discussion of the issue is likely to be heard further up the chain of command.

Everyone I have spoken to with experience in this scenario advises keeping a detailed record of the toxic leader's behavior, all of their excesses, tantrums, and attacks, including, once again, as many witness statements as possible. In barrack room language they call this the 'Asshole Diary.' This is very important, because an Inspector General's report needs to be backed up by evidence, and a he-said-she-said-I-said complaint to the office of the Inspector General will probably not be taken seriously. If there is any investigation at all, it will simply be to contact the offending leader and record his or her denial of every accusation. So, again, keep a detailed record of every incident that you feel crosses the line, including witnesses wherever possible. Remember, what must be proven is *a pattern of behavior*, and not just the irritation of a person having a bad day. Cases that involve multiple complainants willing to give sworn statements carry far more weight than a single accuser.

Remember too, that your case has to be strong. Anonymous complaints usually get nowhere, and hearsay is wasting everyone's time. The military is an environment where authority and leadership are essential to the fabric of the organization, and the establishment will not easily take the side of a subordinate against a leader without a compelling case. As George Reed remarked:

"The system of superordination and subordination is reinforced by both culture and legal code. Leadership might well be a voluntary process in theory, but withholding followership is not a healthy option for most service members."

Article 94 of the Uniform Code of Military Justice, as we have heard already, is clear when it comes to mutiny or any real or perceived insubordination while in uniform. The fact that, at its most severe, the punishment for mutiny is death, should give you an idea of how seriously it is taken.

The advice your father gave you about standing up to bullies in the playground is not the best advice on the parade ground. Any sort of public display of resistance or non-compliance is not going to help your cause, no matter how passionate you might feel about it. Taking a swing at a superior officer will be a one-way ticket to a court martial and a dishonorable discharge, and then you can kiss goodbye to all of your VA benefits. A toxic or destructive leader will see that as insubordination, and the full weight of that person's influence in the chain of command will be brought to bear to destroy you. In the civilian world (theoretically at least) you will have a human resources officer to take up issues of toxicity in the workplace. No such facility exists for the folks in uniform. Discipline is the holy grail of military life, and insubordination is utter heresy.

If confrontation does become the only option, then *do not* do it in public, or in any setting that is likely to cause embarrassment for that person. Schedule a meeting behind closed doors, and present your case in clear, unemotional terms, relying on the reason and integrity of your leader. If your leader proves themselves to have no reason or integrity, which is the exception rather than the rule, then a more nuclear option might become necessary, but be warned, by then the cat will truly be out of the bag.

Indeed, all of the experts on toxic leadership that I consulted with in preparing this book noted that irredeemable malignancy is rare. Actually, in most cases, a leader might not be aware that they are behaving like an asshole, and if the matter is pre-sented to them reasonably and respectfully, they will adjust their behavior accordingly. Like most types of behavior, toxic leadership exists on a spectrum, from a mildly irritable sergeant major who should be avoided before his morning coffee to the sociopathic destroyer of souls. Part of being a good subordinate is to communicate with your commander, and if your instincts tell you that a mild intervention might be fruitful for both sides, then go ahead and do it, just make sure you deploy tact and sensitivity. If your instincts tell you that it will be a waste of time, or worse, that it will blow back on you in a negative way, then don't waste your time.

Something that I have heard time and again is *never* vent, *never* talk trash about a toxic commander to your peers, and *never* to your subordinates. It will get back to the toxic leader, they will take umbrage, and your situation will get a whole lot worse. Divert your anger and irritation to your notebook. Keep a clear and detailed record, and when the time comes, take up the issue with the chain of command or the IG.

When I was deep in my own situation, I was in a place of such anxiety and hell that I could hardly write, and do much of what I am telling you right now.

Sometimes a toxic leader gains some sort of satisfaction in getting under your skin, and so refusing to rise to the bait or maintaining a calm detachment can drive that leader to even greater cruelty and unreasonableness, so sometimes you just cannot win. Now and again an individual will attract the particular ire of a commander, who then takes delight in trying to create as much emotional harm as possible. At times like that, take a pragmatic position. Pick your battles. Strategize to spend as little time under the direction of that individual as possible. Think about training programs or courses that will take you out of the frame for periods, which is just treading water until the metabolism of the military recycles that commander elsewhere. It's a coping strategy, not a solution, and all you are achieving is "passing the trash", and leaving some other poor sap downrange to deal with the shit.

You can draw comfort from the fact that truly destructive toxicity will eventually be noticed. While that individual may not suffer anything as dramatic as a relief of command, they might be tucked away somewhere where they can do no harm, maybe inside of a cubicle at the Pentagon, and be allowed to finish their time and collect their benefits without creating too much of a stir. Sometimes, though, if that individual is highly functional, ambitious, and goal-driven, as many narcissists are, then they are retained because, despite a certain amount of unpleasantness in their wake, they get the job done, and that looks good for their commanders. You can also take comfort from the fact that what goes around often comes around, and most toxic leaders will self-destruct, eventually. Bright lights always cast dark shadows, but they also burn out quickly.

Finally, sometimes what is the easiest and safest route for the victim of a toxic leader is not necessarily the best thing for the organization as a whole. I have run into many stories of individuals who could have kept a low profile and passed the trash, but who took the long view, and realizing that they might be dealing with an individual whose poor leadership qualities are potentially dangerous, took action. To do so takes guts, and the odds of succeeding are usually not excellent.

In most cases, a victim is not likely to be dealing with toxic, incompetent, or dangerous leadership in the middle of a heated battle or a grueling campaign, but in the routine, day-to-day life of soldiering in peacetime. There are plenty of examples in popular literature of commanders being relieved of their command during a crisis, with the mutineers then being faced with a court-martial, to then try and explain to a panel of soft-bodied staff officers what the exigencies were in the fierce flames of battle. Sitting in a witness box trying to explain yourself to a body conditioned to support leadership is an uphill battle at best. Another variable is the possibility that fellow officers and subordinates might support action against a commander when bullets are flying and death is the likely result of a poor decision, but then withdraw that support when facing a court-martial, taking the position "Well I told him not to do it!"

The lesson in this is that the military establishment is by default protective of the command structure, and cognizant of the importance of supporting it. It takes a significant effort, considerable personal risk, and a great deal of resilience to effectively take on a toxic leader, through either the chain of command or the office of the Inspector General, and hope to succeed. It has happened, often, that a commander is relieved, but it is still the exception rather than the rule. Likewise, although it might happen, don't expect your toxic leader to have the scales fall from his eyes, drop to his knees, and tearfully acknowledge his toxic ways. Likely they will fight to the very end, and beyond, to quash the allegations, and if they succeed, they will kick your sorry ass to Sunday.

SO THE QUESTION IS, HOW TO approach a formal complaint? Well, the advice that you are likely to receive, most notably the office of the IG itself, is to take it up first with the chain of command. What this means is going over the head of the toxic leader, which is always risky. It is mandated in the regulations that no soldier making such a complaint should suffer any retribution, but understand that the leader in question will be made aware of the complaint, will likely be able to guess its source, and with the power to make life damned difficult for you, they will sure do their best to do just that.

Also, do not assume that your boss's boss will recognize the point you are trying to make. Remember the 'kiss-up-kick-down' principle. Toxic leaders often look a lot better from the top down than they do from the bottom up, and once they are vindicated, and once they know who initiated the complaint, you will be on the top of that toxic leader's shitlist. If possible, issue a group complaint, which will dilute the focus of an irritated leader if the issue for whatever reason does not gain any traction.

Another point to bear in mind is that toxic leaders very rarely have that self-image. They do not see themselves as toxic, but often as strong and assertive leaders with passion and ambition. Every instance of pushback from an accused toxic leader that I read was about that. It will often be said in reply that it is the malingerers and low achievers who are usually the first to complain (which is often true), and the loudest to do so. And once again, toxic individuals are very often high achievers who climb through the ranks real quick, and gain command positions based on their proven track record, and claims that they are being misjudged or unfairly targeted will very often gain sympathy higher up the chain of command. While the truly malicious sociopath is easy to identify, and will self-destruct sooner rather than later, the borderline toxic can sometimes survive in the institution for the entirety of a career.

If you are unfortunate enough to be confronted by one of those true sociopaths who understand that their behavior is toxic but do not care, then you have a pretty unique problem. Appealing to their better nature is not going to work. Often they feel that their behavior has been validated by their rapid rise through the ranks, their excellent evaluations, and the generally high regard that they are held in by appreciative senior commanders. They will, as a matter of routine, reject the results of any climate assessments, they will certainly not be receptive to feedback from subordinates, and they will not avail themselves of any leadership courses or workshops that might help correct their approach.

IF YOU HAVE A BEEF, AND YOU take it up with the commander, that commander is obligated to undertake an inquiry. Typically the first moves will be informal. For example, as a company commander, I would normally just reach over to the Executive Officer and say, "I want you to go and conduct an informal inquiry about this situation," and I'd leave it to him to run with it. If it turned out that there was a whole lot of smoke hanging around, I'd start to realistically suspect a fire. Then I would prepare a list of possible questions to put to the complainant or complainants, and I'd run those by a JAG officer before any interviews.

Everything you do will have to be written up and will be subject to review, and if your questions are leading, or if they are not correctly phrased, you can sink the whole investigation. Then I would go find both the person that I thought would be *most* likely to cooperate and the person I thought would be *least* likely to cooperate. I would contact them ahead of time, and say – "I will be interviewing you in about a week concerning this issue, and I'll be asking you some questions."

Generally, what I would do is ask them a few questions, and I would make notes, and then I would immediately follow it up with an email containing *my* interpretation of what they said.

"This is what I interpreted our conversation to be, please get back to me within ten days with any corrections and modifications, or anything that needs to be changed."

And that's typically when the rubber starts hitting the road. If they are just running their mouths off with a bunch of lies, and when you start putting that shit on paper, they may want to make a false allegation, but they'll never want to be caught in a lie on paper. If I write it all down and send it to them and ask for their corrections, and they cease to cooperate, then that is as good as gold right there. I've already got them. You have to give them a reasonable amount of time, say a week or two weeks, and if they don't get back to me, then I will give them one follow-up. If they don't correct the record, I will make the necessary assumption, and submit my report.

FROM THIS YOU CAN PROBABLY READ that a senior commander is programmed to disprove allegations, or at least challenge or test them, so heed the ongoing advice to make sure you have a detailed record with receipts and witnesses to back up any issues you may raise.

The other piece of advice that can never be repeated too many times is to try and deal with any issues through the chain of command *before* you make contact with the Office of IG, and definitely before contacting your congressional representative. Here is what a friend, a full colonel said about that:

"So what I used to tell soldiers is, hey, you got a beef, deal with it through the chain of command, because if you go to the IG, or write to your congressman, it is going to come right back to [the chain of command], and we're going to have to do the same thing, but it is going take you another month or two to get your answer."

Dealing with the Inspector General is usually the follow-on option if the chain of command proves unresponsive, or unsatisfactory in its response. Dealing with the Inspector General is usually the follow-on option if the chain of command proves unresponsive, or unsatisfactory in response. Mostly, the Office of the IG is concerned with higher-level allegations, or violations of the law, regulations, or general policy. Although personality clashes or simple disagreements do not warrant the commencement of an investigation, provable cases of cruelty, malignancy, and abuse certainly do. In the case of a criminal complaint, the police would likely have jurisdiction, but more likely, the Air Force Office of Special Investigations, Naval Criminal Investigative Service, or United States Army Criminal Investigation Command, depending on how severe the charges are.

A FREQUENTLY OVERLOOKED AVENUE OF REDRESS is the Article 138 complaint process. According to Article 138 of the Uniform Code of Military Justice: *An Article 138 complaint is a process by which you can attempt to remedy a wrong committed against you by your commanding officer. A 'wrong' may be an action the commander has taken (an act), or the failure of the commander to take an action that should have been taken (an omission). A 'wrong' is something that affects you personally, and is either in violation of a law or regulation, beyond the legitimate authority of the commander, an arbitrary act or an abuse of the commander's discretion, or materially unfair. The 'wrong' may be a deprivation, restriction, or limitation of any right, privilege, benefit, or entitlement.*

The main drawback of an Article 138 complaint, most often described as a 'request for redress', is that it must be submitted in writing to the chain of command, which means that there is no option for anonymity. Typically, a commander has fifteen days from receipt to respond to your complaint, during which they may accept or deny your request. If your request for redress is refused, then the next step in the process is to pursue a formal Article 138 complaint. What this involves is a submission containing the following information:

- Statement that you are a member of the Armed Forces on active duty (or a reservist on inactive duty for training and subject to the UCMJ),
- Your current military organization and unit address,
- Your military organization and unit address at the time the wrong was committed against you,
- The name of the commanding officer who wronged you,
- The date you submitted a request for redress to the commander and a statement that the commander either refused it outright or failed to provide a final response within 15 days,

- A statement that your complaint is submitted under the provisions of Article 138, UCMJ, and Army Regulation 27-10,
- A clear explanation of the complaint, including why you believe the commander's action or inaction is a wrong, and
- A statement of the specific remedial action you seek and why you consider it appropriate.

Attach to this a cover letter and all supporting documents, and then deliver it to your immediate superior commissioned officer in the chain of command within ninety days of discovering the issue at the root of the complaint. That officer must immediately forward the packet to the officer exercising general court-martial jurisdiction, who is typically your commanding general. The matter will then be thoroughly investigated through the chain of command, and if that investigation turns up a legitimate complaint, redress will be forthcoming, and if not, then it will be denied. If the issue is beyond the authority of your commanding general, a review will be undertaken on behalf of the Secretary of the Army, by the office of the Judge Advocate General, and the results of that will be communicated to you.

If you are considering an Article 138 complaint, I would urge you to read the full text of the article which is contained in an appendix at the end of this book. There are several situations where an Article 138 complaint is inappropriate, and those mostly have to do with issues that are already under review in some other area, be it a court-martial, an IG complaint, or an internal process already in motion through the chain of command. If you do decide to go the Article 138 route, get the help of a legal officer to assisting preparing your documentation and drafting your complaint. It is a serious avenue, so make sure you are serious, and that you have all of your ducks in a row.

WHAT ALL OF THIS SHOULD TELL YOU is that there are remedial actions and processes built into the institution to deal with toxic command. The United States military machine is awesome in its scale and scope, but it can sometimes be faceless and inhuman, and possibly those generic systems do not provide any help or relief. Many times in the military you are a number and not a name.

At some point in any career, a soldier in any unit is likely to come up against an asshole leader. It would be a miracle if, in the scope of the full term, a soldier did not, at least once, but likely more than once, run into such a person. I did, more than once, and I also had to cope with a few assholes among my subordinate officers, and I was involved in an investigation. There is no one-size-fits-all solution, but the thing to remember is that you are not alone, there is support out there, and if you play your hand carefully, you can find redress if your case is severe and sincere.

THE OFFICE OF THE INSPECTOR GENERAL

All soldiers have the right to present complaints, grievances, or requests for assistance to the Inspector General. These complaints or grievances may include what Soldiers reasonably believe to be evidence of fraud, waste, and abuse.

Memorandum for All Soldiers, Department of the Army

I HAD A COUPLE OF BRUSHES WITH the office of the Inspector General during my career, the second of which was the more orthodox, insofar as an IG's report was submitted by my executive officer during a combat deployment to Afghanistan in 2011-2012. Although it was kind of an odd situation, it was also in some ways quite common. As I have already noted, I was placed in command of a small preventive medicine detachment, the 452nd Medical Detachment, a reserve outfit out of Perrine, Florida, for deployment to Afghanistan. This was my first combat command, and I took it very seriously.

During my career, I developed a hands-off leadership style, in the belief and understanding that the training my people had received before deployment was enough for them to do their jobs without needing me to be breathing down their necks at all times. During that deployment, I had a great first sergeant, a female NCO by the name of Melisha Palmer, whom I first met on deployment in 1998 in El Salvador during the emergency operation related to Hurricane *Mitch*. Sergeant Palmer took care of a lot of the detailed work that might have sunk me as a commander, and I was supremely grateful for her support during that operation. Subordinate to her was another excellent NCO, Sergeant Yira Rodriquez, who worked under my executive officer, a certain Reserve Captain José Vasquez. It was Captain Vasquez who turned out to be the fly in the ointment of an otherwise flawless deployment.

Captain Vasquez had been led to believe that he would command the unit in Afghanistan, and he was pissed when an active-service officer was seconded in ahead of him. His initial response was to try and insert himself into the command process, and undermine my authority, which failed because, in the end, we just bypassed him. That irritated him even more, and he responded by undermining the unit and making himself as disagreeable as possible. This impacted Sergeant Rodriquez most directly because she served in a remote location as his immediate subordinate. He was counseled, by myself, and he was spoken to and he was advised, but in the end, he was shipped out a month early for reasons superficially of ill health. I call that passing the trash. A point I remember is that Captain Vasquez talked gloriously about the IG process in previous problems he had.

Inevitably, an IG complaint was submitted, complaining essentially of racism and victimization, and after a superficial investigation, the issue was filed away and disappeared. In my opinion, Captain Vasquez was a deeply troubled individual with a malignant streak (I am sure a psychiatrist could probably elucidate this better than me), and it seems that alcohol was part of the picture. However, as is so often the case, he survived this, and other problematic deployments, ending his career as a major with an honorable discharge.

An earlier brush with the office of the IG is maybe more interesting. It happened during my third deployment to Korea, concerning the incident that I have already mentioned. I ran into that turf battle waged by a couple of senior personnel who wanted me out, and they sunk pretty low to achieve that. I was named initially as a pedophile, and rumors were stirred up against me, and then I was identified as a spy, or a security risk at the very least, thanks to my tendency to fraternize and interact with local Korean people. Although both issues were serious, neither of them went anywhere. The truth is, it is very easy to foul up someone's world with vague and unprovable accusations, and then just wait for the stink to make its way up the chain of command. That, however, was nothing more than trouble-making. To get something more tangible, and prosecutable, they tried to get into my computer.

One morning, I bumped into the IG of the 18th MED-COM, in Korea, who commented to me in passing – "Hey, Jason, don't forget to put your CAC into your computer when you log in today."

A CAC is a Common Access Card, which is a general security pass for cyber access, and at the time I thought that was a very strange thing to say because doing it was standard doctrine. In retrospect, what I now understand, is that he was passing me a cryptic warning that someone was trying to gain access to my computer. He had probably picked up some kind of intel, understood through experience that the issue was likely vendetta-driven, and gave me a heads-up. Soon after that my computer crashed and the tech guys could not figure it out. You have always got to be watching your six o'clock when stuff like that is happening. That is usually where it will come from.

THE OFFICE OF THE INSPECTOR GENERAL is an important tool in the arsenal of military personnel management, and in fact, I have often heard it referred to as the Human Resources Department of the Uniformed Services. It has many functions, and for a more detailed overview of this, I would refer you to *Army Regulation 20-1: Inspector General Activities and Procedures*.

For most soldiers, the Inspector General offers an avenue of redress for grievances, and to report any serious malfeasance, corruption, or criminality within the chain of command. Very few senior officers survive a full career without brushing up against the IG a few times. For some it can result in being relieved of command, for others a rebuke or some kind of counseling, but for most just the irritation of having to deal with a malcontented soldier nursing a grievance, or in some way ignorant of standard process and procedure.

Nonetheless, according to the official documentation, "The IG acts as the eyes, ears, voice, and conscience of the commander. The role of the Inspector General and his or her staff is to determine and report on the economy, efficiency, discipline, morale, *esprit de corps*, readiness, and resources of the command."

That is a wide remit, but in layman's terms, every soldier who has a valid concern enjoys the right to avail him or herself of the services of the IG. The process of submitting an IG complaint is pretty simple, and can either be done directly through a hotline number or electronically via a detailed online form. The reality is, though, that the IG will inevitably advise you as a matter of policy to seek initial redress through the chain of command. This is a very important point. The IG will always ask as an opening query whether you have worked with your chain of command to resolve your issue, *but they can't refuse a complaint if the answer is no.* The regulations make all of this clear, and it is worth taking note.

"As a general rule, IGs will encourage the Soldier or Civilian employee to discuss any issues, allegations, or requests for assistance first with the commander, chain of command, or supervisor as provided in AR 600–20. Allowing the chain of command to handle the matter underscores the chain of command's importance and credibility. If the complainant agrees to take an allegation to the chain of command first, and the IG is fully aware of the nature of that allegation, then the IG will follow up with the complainant within five days to ensure that the individual presented it to the chain of command. If the complainant chooses not to bring the allegation to the chain of command's attention, the IG will then accept the allegation into the IG system and refer it to the command or resolve it within the IG system as directed by the appropriate directing authority."[14]

There is good reason for this. In preparation for this book, I chatted with several people with real experience, and I received quite a lot of varied feedback. One particular acquaintance, who commanded at a battalion level, summarized it very well:

"The Inspector General is not some independent, all-powerful, saintly entity that is there to solve all of your problems. If you believe that then you are a fool.

---

[14] AR 20-1 para 6-1b

In fact, the IG works with the commander, within the chain of command, and has four essential functions. Those are, to teach and train, carry out inspections, assist, and implement investigations. Don't get me wrong, the IG can be very useful, and they can wield a lot of influence, but in the world of the common soldier, they usually just hand out generic advice, and move on. If you are dealing with a real toxic commander, or even a senior NCO, then bringing the IG on board as an additional counsel might have some value. But for most issues, it probably makes more sense to just talk with your CoC directly. The bottom line is that the IG is definitely a tool for conflict resolution with really toxic leaders, but the best advice I can give is to use the system sparingly, and wisely."

The office of the IG, across the spectrum of the uniformed services has, over the years, developed a healthy skepticism over most complaints submitted for its consideration. I once spoke to a lawyer who told me that every damn client who does not like the advice on the table submits a bar complaint, which requires the bar to investigate. Bar complaints are always a bit of a black mark on an attorney's record, even though most of the time they turn out to be both spurious and vendetta-driven. The same is true for the IG. In most cases, they will approach a complaint against a commanding officer or NCO cautiously, with a predisposition to write it off as specious.

That was the case regarding my toxic executive officer in Afghanistan, and when I was contacted by the IG to explain my side of the story, it took very little to convince the investigating officer that Vasquez was indeed toxic and that his complaint was without substance. I spoke to another colleague, a battalion commander, who related the story of a soldier who submitted an IG complaint over the fact that his CO was holding on to a school packet that required the signature of the brigade commander. A telephone call was made, and it was established that the brigade commander was on a month-long furlough, and the case was closed.

"I was disappointed to have to answer to an IG investigation," he told me, "but even more disappointed that that soldier did not just come straight to me, or his first line NCO, to ask for clarification."

Sometimes, submitting a claim to the IG can have unintended consequences. Even if the complaint is anonymous, the IG will refer it to the chain of command, and it is usually not difficult to figure out who is at the root of it, and there can be ramifications. For a while, I was stationed at the Defense Logistics Agency at Fort Belvoir, Virginia, and during that period, I was asked to investigate certain allegations, made through a whistleblower channel, of various institutional irregularities within the federal policing agency at Fort Belvoir. The complaints involved nepotism, doctoring fire drill results, and the use of bomb detection mirrors to look up women's skirts. It took me no time at all to figure out who was at the root of the complaints, and it was clear to me that we were dealing a malcontented uniformed member trying to stir up trouble. I guess the furor created by an investigation was enough satisfaction, and when I reported back that I could find no evidence of irregularities, the whole issue disappeared. I'm sure I was not the only one who suspected strongly who was at the bottom of the complaint, and I am sure natural justice did the rest.

On a personal and professional level I really enjoyed that investigation. Many people were coming up to me and asking me out for lunch, and people were giving me all of their attention. Although this was a sensitive issue and was supposed to be hush-hush, word did get out. Once the investigation was over, though, no one invited me out to lunch again.

I recall a story concerning a company suffering under the authority of a particularly atrocious 1st Sergeant, who knew he was a bastard, knew that he was despised, and enjoyed it. A well-researched, supported, and documented IG complaint was submitted, and to the joy of the unit, one day the sergeant held a formation and announced that he had been relieved of command. He expressed his regret, remarking that it had been his life's ambition to lead men, and he said his farewells.

It was a trick, because the next day, he was back, laughing his ass off, telling his men that the IG was worth shit, would and could do nothing, and that now the whole squad was on his shitlist...and so it went.

Another story I recall, told to me by a senior NCO, related to how he was part of an IG process that succeeded and ultimately ended up changing Army regulations. That can be regarded as a successful result.

However, the moral of the story is that, while an IG complaint is often the first line of attack for a disgruntled soldier, and can often be more annoying than substantive, it can also be a powerful force for justice and change if it is properly handled. Another valued contributor to this book, who was involved in multiple command positions, and was also involved in many investigations, gave me his take on the whole process, and a few insider tips, which I will try to summarize.

The reality is that the office of the IG has to sift through a good number of specious complaints to get to the one or two that have substance. "Don't fly off the handle!" I was told. This is advice I have heard time and again. "Make sure you allow things to solidify before making a complaint. You need to have a lot of substance to your complaint."

In my situation, I knew that I was a weakened or compromised person because I did not know how to write or generally understand things well because of the stress of a toxic situation. Keep in mind that if you are the victim of a toxic leader you are probably at one of the worst points in your life, and to be able to successfully defend yourself is going to take a lot of effort and resolve.

Everyone that I have spoken to so far has repeated that same mantra. *"Document and record!"*

Do not make an IG complaint, or even a petition to your congressional representative, without having receipts, detailed documentation, and witnesses.

"You want to make sure that you have a concrete case that does not just rely on I-said-you-said-she-said-he-said because that makes it very difficult for an investigation to pin anything down, and a complaint will usually be filed away in the 'not-to-be-taken-seriously' tray. A phone call might follow, but the case will likely be closed pretty soon."

A point worth bearing in mind as you approach the submission of your IG complaint is that, under the general rules of administrative procedure, the standard of proof is a *preponderance* of the evidence, which is generally interpreted as fifty-one percent, or *more likely than not*. So, once again, the more defensible evidence that you put forward, the better.

If a complaint made through either the chain of command or the office of the IG turns up no result, then a soldier enjoys the right to petition their representative. Congress will then send it over to the

Pentagon with a cover letter attached, after which it makes its way down every level of the chain of command until it arrives on the desk of the supervisor of the individual making the complaint. Then it goes back up, and everyone in between gets to review it, and if they don't like what they see, they send it back down for more information. And so it goes.

Finally, before you pick up the phone and set an IG complaint in motion, look in the mirror, and make sure that *you* are not the problem.

Toxic Leadership and Law Enforcement

I think that we can all agree that a leader doesn't need to necessarily have a title, and having a title doesn't necessarily make you a leader.

Ashlie Walton

A T THE TIME OF WRITING, Derek Chauvin, the Minneapolis police officer at the center of the George Floyd incident that sparked international outrage, was stabbed twenty times by a fellow inmate at Tucson Arizona prison. He survived the attack but was hospitalized with very serious injuries, and his attacker was charged with attempted murder.

Regardless of the symbolism involved in his case, and the nature of what took place, very few military and law enforcement members that I spoke to were inclined to celebrate Derek Chauvin's downfall, and the future that he faces in the prison system. Most, while anxious not to be named, pointed to the Derek Chauvin case as an example of the systemic leadership failures that have come to characterize modern policing in the

United States. Evidence of that was the sudden spike in retirements and medical absences that followed the events that engulfed Minneapolis, and many other cities, in the spring and summer of 2020. The most common story that I have heard concerning that episode is the abandonment of the Minneapolis 3rd Precinct amid the riots and the chaotic and irresponsible manner in which the withdrawal was executed.

The George Floyd killing is a matter of public record, widely reported on, and well known, so we need not dig into that in any detail. However, by the early evening of the day following his death, signs of unrest were noted by the MPD, the focus of which centered on the 3rd Precinct. As the evening progressed, the level of violence around the Precinct grew, as rioters attacked perimeter fencing, broke windows in the building, and vandalized and spray-painted police vehicles. Looting was also beginning to break out in surrounding businesses. Rioting and unrest escalated over the next few days as the 3rd Precinct was increasingly under siege. On the evening of May 28, MPD Police Chief Medaria Arradondo ordered the abandonment and evacuation of the 3rd Precinct. Those officers remaining were stranded in the parking area and were forced to crash the gate with a squad car to get out. Some left the precinct in police vehicles while others left on foot. They regrouped in a warehouse on Hiawatha Avenue where they waited to be collected by buses. Rioters immediately overran the 3rd Precinct building and set fire to it, setting fire also to other buildings in the area.

The evacuation of the 3rd Precinct – some news outlets preferred the term 'the surrender of the 3rd Precinct', placing it in a war-like context – was orderly and controlled, but it was nonetheless terrifying as several officers were forced to make their way through hostile crowds, under assault by rocks, fireworks, pepper spray, fists, and boots. A feeling that the men and women of the Precinct had been abandoned by their superiors began to gather momentum, and a pervasive disillusionment grew. This was the culmination of a sentiment that had been on the boil for some time, and it was confirmed in the minds of many as Derek Chauvin, an imperfect police officer to be sure, was demonized as a symbol of all things wrong with American law enforcement. It seemed to a lot of folks that he was thrown to the wolves to appease the ideological wing of city government, the desire of the police leadership to cover their backs, and the national government in its efforts to appease and placate an ideological wing of the Democratic Party that was demanding the abolition of the police.

While it is not my business to offer any political views or pronouncements, it is difficult not to see all of this as a failure of leadership, and the manifestation of that general view of things was the mass resignations that followed, and the bleeding of urban police departments nationwide.

This, of course, does not represent toxic leadership in the sense that we have discussed so far, which we have defined as the experiences of an individual or unit under the destructive leadership of a particular commander. This is more the institutional failure of an entire leadership structure. It would be similar in effect to serving under an entire toxic chain of command rather than a single toxic officer.

There is a key difference between the police, on the one hand, and military and corporate hierarchies on the other. That difference is simply that the police, as a branch of the uniformed services, interact on a daily basis with the general public, often under high pressure circumstances. Very rarely is the military ever called upon to deal robustly with ordinary citizens, so, while sections of the general public may hold ideological views that are negative, or antithetical to the military, rarely does that have any real bearing on the function of the chain of command. The daily function of police, however, is subject to the vicissitudes of ideology, and as the higher leadership attempt to navigate those unpredictable political waters, they often appear inclined to sacrifice the wellbeing of their serving officers in the interests of protecting their own careers.

Minneapolis Mayor Jacob Frey, along with many other liberal mayors, stood at the forefront of the Defund the Police movement, and could not, as a consequence, be said to have the best interests of individual police officers in mind. Imagine if the President of the United States, the Commander-in-Chief of the armed forces, stood thumping the table, loudly vilifying the serving men and women under his command, and demanding the dissolution of their institution? Senior police administrators, forced to function within this highly politicized environment also tended to protect their careers by throwing the cops on the street under a bus. It was Frey's decision, taken in concert with Chief Medaria Arradondo, that resulted in the abandonment of the 3rd Precinct, and the practical abandonment of the individuals within it.

One of the contributors to this book was Ashlie Walton, who is described as a *First Responder/Armed Service Coach*, with a particular interest in the careers and well-being of first responders. In our discussion on the subject of toxic leadership within law enforcement, it was she who pointed at the events in Minneapolis during that period as, not only an abject failure on the part of the city and police leadership, but one that put the lives of serving officers on the line.

"I have just talked to an officer." She told me. "...who had that experience, who literally left on foot. Imagine being in a literal war zone, without backup, without support, surrounded by people who are armed, who are setting fires everywhere, breaking everything, and you are walking on foot into the middle of it. And not only that, it was the law-breakers enjoying the vocal support of your own leadership! There were a few officers who were in patrol vehicles, but most were on foot, probably dozens, literally walking and running for their lives.

All of those officers were in a state of shock, that they were being given an order like that, to abandon the 3rd Precinct, because that goes against every grain of why they became a first responder in the first place."

She went on to observe that personnel levels in the MPD dropped almost overnight from around eight hundred to around five hundred, a fact reflected in police departments country-wide. Most human resource sources that I contacted took the view that departments countrywide were appalled at the events surrounding the death of George Floyd, but would not be drawn to discuss any failures associated with the treatment *of* the police, but only *by* the police, and reiterating that phycological services are available to any police officer who suffered trauma consequent to the decisions made at a command level.

The question then is how does a police officer deal with concerns regarding leadership in an environment where very little real concern is expressed for the stresses associated with policing and only the excesses attributed to racist policing practices? Although military personnel still enjoy the wide respect and affection of the public, police departments in large parts of the country, in particular in liberal cities, generally do not. What this distills down to is a lack of support, and an ideological decision-making process, a fact that has a singularly negative bearing on an average uniformed police officer.

Can one affect a complaint through Human Resources, I asked, or by submitting a complaint through your congressional representative? Ashlie smiled, shaking her head.

"One hundred percent you will be stigmatized for the rest of your career." She said. "There is no such thing as confidentiality in law enforcement, and it is unlikely that it will be investigated if the complaint is anonymous. Again, it is the overarching ideology that colors everything related to the police. A cop is suffering, great, let him suffer!"

Instead, the advice was simply to change departments. At the time of writing, San Francisco, by now aware of the practical ramifications of a depleted police force, was offering a $70,000 sign-on bonus for qualified personnel. Many other towns and cities are doing likewise. Indeed, hundreds of smaller police departments countrywide are recruiting trained people, and there are currently more openings across the spectrum than people are willing to sign up for. According to many of the folk I spoke to about this issue, there are communities out there that still revere and respect their police officers, so if you working for a department and political establishment that is toxic, the best decision you can make is to make a change.

AS A CONCLUDING NOTE TO THIS BRIEF CHAPTER, many former police officers who left the blue line consequent to these events have entered politics at a local level, placing themselves in a position to lead with a more coherent understanding of the challenges faced by cops on the street. It has also come out in the wash that, while the defund the police movement temporarily resulted in police budgets being slashed, that has, in the intervening period, been quietly reversed. Nonetheless, the effect of it lingers in the ranks of the blue line.

One particular ex-cop who I spoke to made the interesting point that the vilification of police by their own civilian leadership will inevitably become a self-fulfilling prophesy. If conditions of service continue to grow more restrictive and disadvantageous, quality personnel will no longer be attracted to the field, forcing city governments to lower the bar, and thus introduce lower quality personnel onto the streets, and so on. Either way, first responders represent a unique and under-reported factor in the great leadership debate, and very likely we will take it on as a unique subject sometime at a later date.

THE PERSPECTIVE OF A MILITARY CHAPLAIN

Here a question arises: whether it is better to be loved than feared, or the reverse. The answer is, of course, that it would be best to be both loved and feared. But since the two rarely come together, anyone compelled to choose will find greater security in being feared than in being loved.

Niccolo Machiavelli

CONFIDENTIALITY IS ONE OF THE CONCERNS that I heard a whole lot about in my conversations with folk dealing with toxic leadership. The military has a tier system of mandatory reporters, whereby Commanders, first sergeants, and supervisors (both military and civilian) are required to move information up their chain of command, and if necessary, notify the Office of Special Investigation. Absolute confidentially in the military is acknowledged only in a few areas, one of which is the Army Judge Advocate General`s Corps, and another is consultation with an Army Chaplain.

Let's have a quick look at who the Chaplain is, and what their job description represents. According to the encyclopedia definition: "A military Chaplain ministers to military personnel and, in most cases, their families and civilians working for the military. In some cases, they will also work with local civilians within a military area of operations."

In the old days, the Corps of Chaplains was dominated by the Christian faith, and in many areas it still is, but these days, an Army Chaplain can be Catholic, Jewish, Orthodox Christian, Muslim, and Protestant, reflecting the diversifying personnel of the United States uniformed services. Chaplains typically enter the service with the rank of captain, for the same reason as a lot of other professionals do, because a basic requirement to join the corps is a Master of Divinity, or similar qualification, and an endorsement by a recognized religious group. In the Christian context, that means ordainment, and in the Jewish and Muslim faiths, to be an ordained Rabbi or Imam. A common observation about this is that the Chaplain will often be the oldest and best educated among the battalion staff, although often not the most militarily astute.

Another interesting detail about Chaplains is that, although they hold rank, and enjoy all of the authority that goes with that, they do not occupy leadership positions, and will never be appointed to a command role. This is all wrapped up in the idea of the separation of church and state, besides which, Chaplains are essentially priests, and a certain implication of non-violence goes with that. Even the highest-ranking Chaplain in the service, who is a two-star general, has no command authority. Typically, a Chaplain, regardless of rank, is addressed as 'Chaplain', with the addition of 'Sir' if appropriate. Chaplains do not carry arms, are non-combatants, are not permitted to direct combat roles, order an assault, or issue directives in combat, even if they are the last surviving officer.

Having said all of that, how is a Chaplain relevant to the subject of this book? The fact that a Chaplain functions in an environment of confidentiality, just like a priest or any other ordained person, liberates them from the responsibility of reporting details up the chain of command. This, of course, means that any conversation with a Chaplain goes no further, and that is very important if a Chaplain is consulted over an issue of command toxicity, the victimization of an individual by his or her commander, and in instances of sexual assault, sexual harassment or any other similar malfeasance. It is also true that the Chaplain enjoys an open door to whichever command they report to, and is thus in a position to approach any senior officer informally and open a discussion on any subject, again within the circle of confidentiality.

Most advice that you will receive, even here in the pages of this book, is to consult the Chaplain before you decide which way to proceed if you have it in mind to pursue a formal complaint. My experience in the military taught me that the chaplain is always easy to talk to. It is the Chaplain's job to offer advice and counsel, and typically a battalion Chaplain has seen most issues, and will probably have the appropriate advice to offer.

One of my chaplain friends serving in the United States Army right now had much thought-provoking material to complement the themes of this book, and also one or two interesting stories. This particular individual joined up later in life, having already pursued his divinity degree, and passed through ordainment, feeling in the aftermath of the 9/11 attacks that it was his duty to offer his service. He was deployed to Iraq in 2006, during combat operations, and he told me the story of his battalion commander, who he was anxious that we not name, but who he called Colonel Mike. Colonel Mike, it seems, had a real bad case of toxic leadership.

"Toxic leadership," My friend the chaplain said, reflecting opinions I had already heard many times, and in diverse quarters, "is all and any style of leadership where a leader's actions are ultimately harmful to both their followers and to the organization. It is characterized by a lack of concern for the well-being of subordinates, and it is often characterized by manipulation, usually driven by fear."

This led us to discuss the Machiavellian principle that, if you cannot be both, it is better to be feared than loved. The years 2006 and 2007 were the deadliest years of the war in Iraq, and it was a harrowing time for everyone involved. Colonel Mike commanded a combat infantry battalion that was in the thick of the action, and during that period he developed a near obsession with ensuring that men serving under his command came out of it alive. His period of combat command was blighted a little by more than one suicide among his troops, and it seems that he was haunted by the responsibility that this placed on him, which in turn seemed to influence his behavior in unexpected ways.

Colonel Mike was described as a bull of a man, north of six feet two, well-built, aggressive, and tireless. According to my friend, who is a highly educated man, Mike showed all the worst characteristics of a Machiavellian prince and precious few of the good.

Chapter 17 of Niccolo Machiavelli's *The Prince* is called *Concerning Cruelty and Clemency, and Whether it is Better to Be Loved than Feared.* In it, there are a few leadership principles that we could recognize in a toxic leader, but they are leavened by other principles that balance out cruelty with compassion. Machiavelli continues:

"Upon this, a question arises: whether it be better to be loved than feared or feared than loved? It may be answered that one should wish to be both, but, because it is difficult to unite them in one person, is much safer to be feared than loved, when, of the two, either must be dispensed with."

Every commander ought to aspire to a reputation for compassion, but in the even balance of love and fear, it might be necessary (at least in a historical context) to execute a few poor souls in the most dramatic way possible as a reminder to the rest of the army that, while the chief can be reasonable and caring most of the time, he can also be brutal and cruel if the circumstances demand it. In an ideal world, that lesson need only be taught once to thereafter sustain a general regime of moderation, empathy, and compassion. That, unfortunately, in the grand scheme of things, seems to be the exception rather than the rule.

In the mission-driven environment of the military, in particular under conditions of combat, as was the case in Iraq during that crucial axis of 2005-2007, there is a strong incentive to deploy that principle of being feared rather than loved because, in the short term, it gets results, it gets troops out alive and it caps off the mission. Most commanders will be looking at twenty-four months, three years maximum, to get the job done and get out. It is very tempting to deploy that tool of fear and intimidation under such circumstances because it gets results. It is also worth remembering that command is an important part of gaining promotion.

There can be an immediate payoff, but also, oftentimes, in the long game, a leader who is loathed and feared will undermine trust and cooperation within the organization, decrease morale, and increase stress. It burns soldiers and subordinates out, with the result that there will be a high turnover rate of folks just exiting the military, and under wartime conditions, sometimes high rates of suicide. According to my Chaplain friend:

IN 2006 THERE WERE MANY SOLDIERS who had multiple deployments under their belts, and Colonel Mike had to deal with a few suicides before the unit was pushed out to deploy to Iraq. That was a first-time life experience for Mike, and I saw the change in his demeanor. His crossover into toxicity as a leader was not driven by the usual need for self-promotion or validation and aggrandizement, but to make sure that he minimized combat fatalities and suicides within his command. He said to himself, "I have to be harder. I need to be more exacting because I need all of my people to be on their toes. I need all of my people to be on their toes, in the game, their heads in the fight, because I do not want to have to do another memorial service. I don't want to lose another soldier."

So, I understand Mike's rationale for reaching toxicity. It was Mike who pointed out Machiavelli to me in a conversation. That became his mantra. It is better to be feared than loved. And he talked about that often. It is better to be feared than loved.

He hoped that if I did this then we would be successful in our mission, and we will be successful in bringing people back alive. I think most of us can`t really argue with that. I think we can look at a commander who desires to be successful in the mission and to bring people back safe and sound is a noble thing, but I think what Mike missed is that there are other leadership styles and other leadership tools that can produce similar outcomes in similar ways.

Certainly, if you are sending troops on a high-stakes assault, you probably need to deploy a little bit of hard power, but the secret of leadership excellence is to understand the balance between ruthlessness and compassion, cruelty and empathy. Mike was so changed by those early events that he went hauling-ass with the fear and intimidation, and he developed a persona intended to instill that fear among his subordinates.

It was difficult to talk to him. As Chaplain, I tried to talk to him, to tell what I was hearing, what was being spoken, but he flung himself out into the hallway, stopped the nearest non-commissioned officer, and asked with a full-throated roar, "Sergeant, I'm hearing that we have a morale problem! Do we have a morale problem?"

And there, in the moment, his eyes wide, the poor guy could only reply, "No Sir!"

Mike tuned back to me and said, "There Chaplain, you see, no morale problem!"

Nonetheless, the role of a Chaplain under such circumstances is mediation. Part of the duties of a Chaplain is to act as a director advisor to the commander. It is not a role that holds any particular authority, or any formality, and a commander can order a Chaplain out of his office as perfunctorily as he can any junior officer, but simply because of his or her spiritual office, a Chaplain enjoys a certain amount of gravity. It could be said that he has God on his side, and the commander would do well to take heed.

COLONEL MIKE'S TOXICITY emerged in the aftermath of the suicides, and clearly, he was affected by that, altered, in fact. In his role as internal advisement, the Chaplain was able to knock on the 'old man's' door and say. "Hey Sir, or Ma'am, here is what I am hearing, here are the issues." And often a frank conversation would follow.

"But Mike was so fearful of losing one more soldier. Here was a man who was being controlled by fear, and in turn using fear to control others."

Mike did not experience another suicide, but suicide ideation grew in the ranks, and visits to the Chaplain increased, along with self-reporting to behavioral health, and as others in the unit became better equipped to recognize the signs to intervene. "If that did not exist." The Chaplain told me. "I am convinced it would have resulted in a whole different picture."

An interesting conclusion to this chapter would be the Chaplain's observation that. while the toxicity of the commander deeply affected unit morale, it advanced the mission, simply because people did not want to get smoked or beat up by the commander. His methodology was textbook, since he berated junior officers in front of the men, used demeaning language, and allowed his ass-chewings to attenuate into criticisms of intelligence and ability way beyond the requirements of the situation. The story was repeated to me of a briefing where a last-minute PowerPoint slide was introduced using a font different from the rest, which prompted a brutal and humiliating outburst of unnecessary insult, cussing, and abuse – over a PowerPoint font!

The fact that all of this played out under conditions of war, and during a series of critical engagements, removing a high-performing commander for reasons of toxicity did not make a whole lot of sense. Although, after fifteen months of it, troop morale, spirit, and mental health were in tatters, it was possible to look back and say that the deployment had been successful. Stellar, in fact, because the unit had accomplished all of its assignments and duties, and ended up receiving a presidential unit citation.

On the tarmac, on the receiving line, as the unit returned stateside, the divisional commander, a two-star general, greeted every soldier with a vigorous handshake. When it came to the turn of the Chaplain, the general embraced him, and whispering in his ear, said, "I heard about it, and I am so sorry Father, so very sorry."

At All Costs

You will never change someone's behavior. What you can change is how you deal with it.

Dr. Jude Black

I FELT THAT I NEEDED TO INCLUDE A CHAPTER dedicated to issues of toxic and destructive leadership in bureaucratic environments other than the military, but as I read through the various books and articles necessary to paint a picture of corporate life, be it in the private sector of government, I was struck by how similar those types of environment are to the military garrison in South Korea. Since I do not have a whole lot of experience in a professional life outside of the military, I figured I would offer up a few more of my own experiences in South Korea before jumping into the details of leadership in the corporate world.

The military garrison in South Korea ranks among the most important U.S. overseas deployments across the whole military spectrum. Why is it so important? Well, the answer to that lies with the lingering tensions that remain after the effective end of the Korean War. In 1953, an armistice was agreed upon between North and South Korea that paused hostilities intending to pursue more formal and permanent peace measures. That peace was never cemented, and so the pause has remained in effect simply as a ceasefire. In formal terms, the two nations remain at war.

The U.S. garrison in South Korea is substantively tasked with the job of deterring any potential attack coming across the DMZ from North Korea, but in reality, it is mainly there to bolster and support the strategic US alliance with South Korea. The Republic of Korea, as it is formally known, is a key U.S. ally in the region, and in the last thirty years or so, that alliance has become less about the old echoes of the Korean War than the necessity for a military counterbalance to the growing regional influence of China. The troop contingent is not huge, standing at just under 29,000, comprising, among others, the U.S. Eighth Army (EUSA), U.S. Air Forces Korea (Seventh Air Force), U.S. Naval Forces Korea (CNFK), U.S. Marine Forces Korea (MARFORK) and U.S. Special Operations Command Korea (SOCKOR).

The net effect of all of this is that a whole lot more diplomatic and military liaison takes place than any combat preparedness. And so a lot, probably a majority, of the functionaries within the military structure in South Korea are not combat troops, but soft-body personnel, comprising various staff, supported by many civilian contractors, and bolstered by a lot of Korean nationals employed by the US military. As a consequence, there is a high concentration of senior rank in a very small operational area, including a three-star command. A lot of ranking people function in a limited space under very senior general command, stepping on each other's toes and getting on each other's nerves, which means that politics tends to be rampant throughout. It reminds me of a lot of rats in a cage, with wicked infighting, a whole lot of competition, back-stabbing, and a shit-ton of competing egos. Add to that the additional stress of folk who work together in very tight conditions, living together just as close, and interacting socially as well as professionally. It is a situation that can get toxic pretty quickly if you are not damn careful.

I began my second tour in South Korea as a newly promoted major, sent over to take command of the 5th Medical Detachment. I was newly married, with an infant daughter, and this was my first command. Commanding another sister detachment, the 38th Medical Detachment (both subordinate to the 168th Medical Battalion), was a female Environmental Science Officer by the name of Major Lynda Lim, who, although not directly in my chain of command, was someone I worked very close to.

She was nothing special to look at, standing maybe five foot two or three, slight at the breast but heavy at the hip, bespectacled, brunette, and with the kind of short hairdo that a lot of female soldiers adopt. There was nothing about her that I would have looked twice at in the corridor of any administrative block, but very quickly I began to hear stories.

The soldiers attached to both of our units bunked in the same barracks, and as soldiers do, they talked about their officers and leaders. The first thing I picked up on was my first sergeant telling the men when they bitched about this or that, that there was another unit just up the corridor that would be glad to take them in if they were unhappy. That was usually enough to shut them up. "Hell no!" was the typical retort, and from that I figured that serving under Major Lim's command was not a happy place to be, and it did not take very long for me to start seeing proof of it with my very own eyes.

On first impression, she seemed friendly and char-ismatic, very mannish in body language, adopting a kind of bluff, companionable, and bantering style that worked well in general male company. Although she was going through a divorce, and had a couple of young kids, the general feeling was that she was gay or bi-sexual. I invited her round to my house once for drinks, and she showed up with a female captain, and it seemed to both Beverly, my wife, and me that they were together. Her female companion, and this is not a joke, was a person whose name was Captain Love. Sometimes Lynda would tell me, "Hey Jason, I'm gonna go get some Love."

Sometimes Major Lim and I would ride down to Camp Walker in Daegu on the train, for a briefing or meeting with our supervisors, and if we traveled with a bunch of soldiers, she would hang out, her legs spread wide open, like men do, scratching herself and talking shit, telling filthy jokes and raising a whole lot of laughs. She was the funniest female I have ever been around.

But then there was another side to her. The ambition, the naked, undisguised ambition, just oozed out of her skin. It scared the shit out of me. There was an intensity about her that was plain scary. I once said to her, as kind of a joke, but really not, that I thought she was a damned narcissist, and she laughed, and replied, "Hell Jason! Have you only just figured that out now?"

One time, after visiting a detachment of U.S. Marines somewhere in South Korea, she told me how impressed she was at the way that Marines regarded their officers. "Hey Jason," She said. "those enlisted people when they get around their officers, they believe that they are sorta like *Gods!*"

That is true. It is part of Marine culture. They have an exaggerated reverence for their officers, and she loved that. She liked the idea of being put on a pedestal and treated like a God. She was a damn narcissist for sure.

I have a hands-off leadership style. I'm laid back, and the problem with me is I might just be too easy. I think it comes from being prior-enlisted, and kind of a good `ole boy. I identify very closely with my soldiers, and I get on well with them as peers. I like to put my faith in diligent training so that when the unit is in the field or on operations the soldiers know exactly what to do without me having to micro-manage anyone. Major Lim, on the other hand, was a wicked micro-manager, and I heard many stories about nuclear explosions going on in her unit, and long, berating, insulting, and demeaning screaming fits, as she got into the faces of her soldiers, and really let rip. She did not seem to be capable of just letting her soldiers do their job, and when they did, she could not help herself but criticize. Often, our conversations, when they happened, would be about the hell she lived in, how everything was always jacked in her unit, how screwed her people were, and what a burden she had to carry to keep the mission on track. Sometimes I felt like advising her to just step back, and let the soldiers do their job, but I figured that would be a waste of time.

And then, of course, there was that other side to her too, one of the typical characteristics of a toxic leader that complicates and confuses the general situation. That fact is she was brilliant. She was very smart. I recall that she could upchuck at a moment's notice the entire manual of military preventive medicine, all of the conventions and regulations, and every conceivable best practice. The Army was her life, every aspect of her waking existence, and she drove herself relentlessly to be the best of the best. One time, a certain colonel visited us in Korea from

Washington D.C. He was an entomologist, a bug doctor, and I guess he came over for some sort of training in Korea. Major Lim invited him for a social evening at her home, making sure before he arrived to clear out all of the kid's toys and replace them with new toys that were all insects. This was what we call a sucking-up measure. That colonel was not in her chain of command and would have no specific influence over any performance assessments that she might have been chasing, but she still went that extra mile to impress him with the fact that her home was filled with toy insects. She wanted to be the best of the best, and I figured that she probably was. I would guess that her superiors and senior officers were wildly impressed by her performance, and since I never recall a word of her kick-down tendencies, it was the kiss-up that really scored for her.

I was also not in her chain of command, but she perceived me as a threat since we were competing for evaluations because we were the same rank. I had a trailer as part of my unit's equipment that we used to haul kit and materials if we were out on an operation or a field exercise, and one day that trailer went missing. I had everybody looking around for it. I even looked around for it myself, everywhere on base, but it was nowhere to be found. I had to report it missing and had to pay for it, and eventually, it became a staff-level action. Although it may not seem like much, it definitely was. Things like that are considered a real bad black mark because what it tells a senior rater is that an officer is unable to keep accountability for his equipment, and that sure is not a good thing.

And then, when the dust settled a little bit, the damn thing reappeared. I got my money back, but the black mark remained. A few years later, on Fort Belvoir, I ran into her at a gas station, and I suggested we grab lunch and catch up. We met at the soldier's canteen, and during the conversation, I mentioned that I was still looking for that trailer, and she gave me a slight grin and a side-eye, I figured that she knew all about that trailer disappearing.

SOUTH KOREA, IN THE YONGSAN GARRISON, functions in many respects just like a corporate bureaucracy, and the cause and effect of destructive leadership is just the same. However, there are a few key differences between military and corporate leadership that might be worth noting here. The main difference lies in varying objectives. In the corporate world, the main objective is profit, while in the military it is national security in an overarching sense, but at a more grassroots level, success in an individual mission, the wellbeing of soldiers, and the general philosophy that service to one's country supersedes individual needs. That is, however, only a philosophy, a guiding principle, because, as illustrated above, individual career advancement certainly does play a huge role in decision-making within a military chain of command, and certainly in the integrity of one's actions towards others.

In other areas, like hierarchy and decision-making, there are also key differences. The military hierarchy is rigid and generally inflexible, reflecting an idea that we have explored often already in this book, that even under circumstances of extreme stress, respect for leadership and adherence to command must prevail. Corporate hierarchies, on the other hand, are much more flexible and dynamic, which, incidentally, is often why old soldiers are not generally preferred for high-ranking corporate appointments. Corporate leadership mainly concerns itself with financial and market risks, and as a rule, they are usually pretty risk-averse. Military leaders obviously deal with extreme risk as a fact of life, and the stakes are considerably higher, so obviously a high standard of discipline is necessary. Military leaders need to pay almost no attention to the broader question of money and are instead promoted according to the metrics of mission accomplishment, discipline, troop morale, and adherence to military regulations. Rarely ever is individual creativity encouraged, let alone rewarded. The corporate metric of revenue growth, profitability, and market share will definitely get a corporate functionary noticed, but it can also lead to toxicity in just the same way as excessive operation zeal can achieve in the military. In terms of leadership style, while military leadership tends to emphasize discipline, obedience, and a command and control style, corporate leadership has to be more flexible and collaborative, but it can also often be just as autocratic and uncompromising as the military.

We know why people stay in the military despite the stresses of toxic leadership, and we have discussed those reasons so often in this book already that we do not need to go back and recapitulate. Many of those essential rationales are evident in numerous studies into why corporate and administrative people also endure years of abusive leadership rather than simply throwing in the towel, and moving on. One time, while I was deployed to El Salvador on Operation *New Horizon*, I got to talking to a UN aid worker from Connecticut who was working with orphaned kids, and even though she despised her local UN coordinator, and dealt with unwanted sexual advances as a matter of routine, she felt that her work in the country was just too important to abandon over issues that she was morally strong enough to handle.

Civilian bureaucratic structures are very different from the military since the rotational dynamic that characterizes military appointments is absent. What that can mean is facing the reality of an open-ended relationship with a bad departmental head or tyrannical supervisor. Possibly an individual living from paycheck to paycheck might not feel empowered to simply walk off the job and start looking for another. The bottom line is that the military and civilian dynamic in being confronted with and dealing with, toxic leadership is mostly the same, at least in terms of stress and that feeling of hopelessness. In some ways, the civilian experience is worse, because there is not the powerful presence of a senior command legally mandated to take any complaint seriously. Human resources departments are theoretically positioned to help, but almost no reports and anecdotal experiences that I read suggest that they help very much.

So what can be done in a civilian bureaucratic environment if toxic leadership becomes an issue? Assuming that you are not in a position to throw your resignation letter down on the table, here are a few suggestions.

In much the same way as the office of the IG will encourage you to take the matter up within the chain of command, it makes sense to try talking first. Avoid confrontation, and certainly avoid violence, and definitely make sure that whatever conversations you have are conducted behind closed doors, and never talked about in the general population. Talking bad about your boss behind their back is never a good idea, word will always get back, and there will be consequences. Do not put anything negative online or on social media at all. Instead, keep it calm and civil, and if that does not work, look around for other opportunities in the organization. In many publications, the advice is to develop a support network within your department or organization, which would be a group of friends who might be in a position to support one another, depending on who is the focus at any given time of the toxic leader.

Generally, if you chose the route of consulting with your HR department, take note of earlier chapters, and make sure you keep a detailed report on your experiences, and as much as possible, back that up with supporting testimony. Chances are that the HR people will know who and what you are talking about, and possibly they would be able to help. Never weaponize your HR department. That runs parallel to the military. Mostly they have seen it all before and they will know what the game is.

Human Resources, however, does not have the kind of muscular resources that the office of the Inspector General does, and it can very often be susceptible to the same types of office politics that motivate the toxic leader. No individual in uniform has a financial stake in the organization. No investments are held, and no stock is owned. However, if the toxic leader you are dealing with is the business owner or partner, then you are screwed. No boss will fire or reassign an individual who is invested in the business over an employee. That is just a fact of life. In a situation like that, you live with it, or you leave, because you will never prevail in an open fight, and HR certainly will not come riding to your rescue, if it ever will.

Some issues will motivate HR to act, even in the case of a very senior member, when credibly accused of racism or sexual malfeasance. However, do not be tempted to throw out false accusations because, while sometimes that might get a result, it will poison the atmosphere, and if they cannot get you on that issue, they'll get you on another.

In the end, what it comes down to is planning your exit. If the situation has become intolerable, then make the decision to move, but in doing so, plan and execute that departure with as much precision as you can. The most important advice that I hear, time and again, is to avoid confrontation. Make sure you have your next job lined up before you leave. Don't burn bridges because you might need a reference. Give proper notice, tick all the boxes, and remember to shake everyone's hand. Keep clean, civil, and disciplined. Remember, be you in a military or civil environment, do not yield to the temptation to slander your previous boss as you are interviewed by your future boss. They might look at you as the problem, and at all costs, in this toxic leadership dynamic, make sure that you are not the problem.

HOW IT AFFECTS YOUR FAMILY

An institutional cancer with the high propensity to metastasize, leaving a path of destruction, poison, and scars...

Dr. Jude Black

IN THIS BRIEF, CONCLUDING CHAPTER, I would like to touch on how toxic leadership affects the family of the person directly experiencing its effects. This, once again, is viewed from the military perspective, but I am quite certain that the same effects are felt across the board. In 2015, a groundbreaking survey was carried out as part of the doctoral thesis of Judith Black, who is now Dr. Judith Black, one of the leading authorities on toxic leadership, exposing the effect of toxic leadership on spouses and families.

This is a very under-examined area of the whole toxic leadership issue, and it does stand to reason that the stresses and difficulties felt in the work environment will spill over into the private lives of those at the receiving end. Readers will recall the story told to me of a sergeant who regularly invaded the home of a subordinate specialist to have his way with the man's wife. That is an extreme example of toxicity at a command level entering the home life of a serving individual. The way that the story was told to me precludes the suspicion that the woman was simply having an affair with the sergeant and rubbing her husband's nose in it. The sergeant was later tried by court-martial on several counts of rape, found guilty, and duly sentenced to a lengthy prison term. Obviously, there is more to this story than rape in the conventional sense of the word, and the sense of entitlement that that individual must have felt is nothing less than epic. The moral of the story is that the specialist felt that he was powerless to stop that behavior, and more importantly, his wife felt no less powerless and succumbed to that treatment because she felt that she had no choice.

Protecting a husband's military career seems to be the reason for the silence and submission of most women included in the survey, which actually involved only ten individuals in a very searching interview process. The ten wives were each stationed with their husbands at different locations around the world, and perhaps the signature takeaway was that each felt that a procedure should be put in place to allow spouses to provide feedback on commanders, since spouses in volunteer leadership positions are supervised by, and receive performance evaluations from those commanders. The risk always is that if a spouse resists or reacts to a toxic commander, the career, or just the day-to-day life of the service member will suffer, or be compromised in some way. One or two of the women interviewed cited clear instances where their husbands suffered directly as a consequence of tension between a spouse and a toxic commander.

Besides that, all ten women reported feelings of help-lessness, anger, frustration, and depression, on top of the natural anxiety and concern they would feel for the difficulties experienced by their husbands. A common volunteer organization in military garrisons is the Family Readiness Group (FRG), a command-sponsored effort. The official description of an FRG is this:

"FRGs are established to provide activities and support to enhance the flow of information, increase the resiliency of unit soldiers and their families, provide practical tools for adjusting to military deployments and separations, and enhance the well-being and esprit de corps within the unit. Since one of the goals of an FRG is to support the military mission through the provision of support, outreach, and information to family members, certain FRG activities are essential and common to all groups, and include member meetings, staff and committee meetings, publication and distribution of newsletters, maintenance of virtual FRG websites, maintenance of updated rosters and readiness information, and member telephone trees and e-mail distribution lists."

When I was deployed to Afghanistan, my wife, Beverly, was the FRG team leader. Most of the time the commander's wives are going to be the FRG leaders while the unit is away on deployment, and I feel this is an essential tool that a lot of military members and spouses can use. FRGs are integral to garrison life and are usually the exclusive reserve of Army wives.

Judith Black's survey cited FRGs as the first casualty of a toxic command environment for the obvious reason that that is the main point of contact between commanders and unit spouses. One spouse reported that she quit her position as an FRG leader after she was threatened by the commander. Others were fearful of being involved in the FRG at all.

Within the confined environment of a military garrison, the stress and difficulties associated with toxic leadership bled into the health of individual marriages, causing break-ups and crises within those marriages, and the residual animosity developed lingered for years after the event. Some wives leave the base altogether, returning home to billet with families for the duration of that commander's presence on base, and certainly, no few marriages have floundered on the rocks of a difficult and stressful work environment.

"That says a lot. I would rather have my husband go away to a combat zone than ever work for a guy like that again. Yeah, it was that bad."[15]

---

[15] Quoted: Military Times. *Effects of Toxic Leadership Could Reach Deep into Families, Research Finds.* Karen Jowers. Nov 12, 2015.

Spouses universally agreed that they could access no help within the Army community for dealing with toxic leaders. Typically they were afraid to seek help from Army support services, and even chaplains, for fear that the toxic leader would discover it, and cause even greater harm. According to the eminent Colonel George Reed (retired), who has contributed so much to this book already:

"It's human nature to pull back, human nature to withdraw, if they feel they're being belittled, humiliated, or if they feel they're being taken advantage of," he said. "I'm a firm believer that the impact of working for a bad boss extends farther than we've realized. We're only beginning to understand how far it extends."

WHAT I HAVE LEARNED FROM WRITING THIS BOOK is what I hope you have learned from reading it. Experiences with toxic leadership and corrosive, destructive leaders, particularly in the military, are often just a fact of life, but rarely is it all of life. I do recall George Reed's observation that excellent leadership across the spectrum is the rule rather than the exception, and even though bad leadership can have a profound impact when you do encounter it, it does tend to be the exception. Remember, that you are not alone, that there are tried and tested methods of dealing with it, and that so long as you follow the basic steps that I have laid out in this book, you will more than likely survive, and thrive. I wish when I was in some of the darkest places of my career I had known what I know now, and I hope y'all out there now know what I did not know then.

If I was to distill it all down to just one simple principle it would be the 'Asshole Diary'. Just the simple fact of keeping detailed notes, and building a solid case, is therapeutic, it clears away that terrible fog of lonely helplessness, and it is the one tool that is difficult for an investigating officer to argue with. Make sure to keep detailed records, gather as many witness statements as you can, and then consider carefully which avenue of attack you are going to take.

It is also perhaps worth reiterating that talking can sometimes take you places that confrontation never will. When I reflect on my experiences at the hand of Colonel (Retired) Ted Small, if I had had enough humility at the time to just give the man what he craved, which was respect for his eminence in an obscure field of entomology, he may not have set about destroying me the way that he did. Perhaps not, but I suspect that I could have nipped the situation in the bud if I had taken a different route myself. That will obviously not be true for everyone, but it is my belief, and the belief of a good number of the experts I spoke to, that most people are empathic and desirous of doing the right thing, and if they are approached in a non-confrontational way, will often endeavor to modify their behavior. If not, and if you have to go to war, make sure that you are well armed and well supported, and make use of all the many avenues available to you to gain redress.

APPENDIX I

Article 138 Information

1. Purpose: **To provide information concerning Article 138 procedures**

2. Facts:

a. AR 27-10, Chapter 19, implements Article 138, UCMJ

b. An Article 138 complaint is a process by which you can attempt to remedy a wrong committed against you by your commanding officer.

A "wrong" may be an action the commander has taken (an act), or the failure of the commander to take an action that should have been taken (an omission). A "wrong" is something that affects you personally, and is either in violation of a law or regulation, beyond the legitimate authority of the commander, an arbitrary act or an abuse of the commander's discretion, or materially unfair. The "wrong" may be a deprivation, restriction, or limitation of any right, privilege, benefit, or entitlement.

Generally, an Article 138 complaint can be used any time you feel a commanding officer has committed a wrong against you. As discussed below, there are some exceptions. Common examples of perceived wrongs are when a commander unreasonably denies your request for leave or revokes promotion orders for unknown reasons.

The Article 138 process is not appropriate when the Army has provided alternative channels for resolving the complaint. Examples include: Complaints relating to a court-martial or Article 15 proceeding; Complaints arising out of most board actions, such as officer or enlisted elimination boards, flight evaluation boards, reduction boards, or formal AR 15-6 investigations; Actions for which Army regulations specifically authorize an administrative appeal (for example, complaints relating to officer or NCO evaluation reports, findings of financial liability as the result of a report of survey, or filing of written reprimands or other adverse information in official personnel records); A commander's recommendation or initiation of an action listed above. For example, if your commander recommends you receive a field grade Article 15 for missing a formation, you may not file an Article 138 complaint.

c. Steps of how Article 138 works:

STEP 1: If you feel you've been wronged and want that wrong "fixed," you must first submit a written request for redress (fixing of the wrong) through your chain of command to the commander who has committed the wrong against you. A request for redress must contain the following information:

(1) Name and unit of the commanding officer against whom you are making the request for redress;

(2) An explanation of the nature of the alleged wrong committed against you;

(3) The remedial action you desire.

STEP 2: The commanding officer normally has 15 days from the date of receipt to respond to your request for redress. If more time is needed, the commander should provide you an interim response indicating the estimated date of the final response. In acting on your request, the commander may take remedial action or refuse your request. If no final response is received within 15 days through no fault of yours (and no interim response has been provided), you may assume your request for redress has been refused.

STEP 3: If the commander refuses your request for redress, the next step is to pursue the matter through a formal Article 138 complaint. An Article 138 complaint must be in writing, signed by you, and contain the following information:

(1) Statement that you are a member of the Armed Forces on active duty (or a reservist on inactive duty for training and subject to the UCMJ),

(2) Your current military organization and unit address,

(3) Your military organization and unit address at the time the wrong was committed against you,

(4) The name of the commanding officer who wronged you,

(5) The date you submitted a request for redress to the commander and a statement that the commander either refused it outright or failed to provide a final response within 15 days,

(6) A statement that your complaint is submitted under the provisions of Article 138, UCMJ, and Army Regulation 27-10,

(7) A clear explanation of the complaint, including why you believe the commander's action or inaction is a wrong, and

(8) A statement of the specific remedial action you seek and why you consider it appropriate.

STEP 4: You must attach to the Article 138 complaint your request for redress to the commanding officer and any supporting information, documents, or statements you want to have considered in support of your Article 138 complaint.

Updated Dec 15

STEP 5: Deliver the Article 138 complaint and all supporting documents to your immediate superior commissioned officer.

d. You must submit an Article 138 complaint to your immediate superior commissioned officer within 90 DAYS from the date you discovered the wrong. The 90-day limit excludes any period of time your request for redress was in the hands of the commanding officer against whom you submitted it. The best advice would be to submit a request for redress to the commanding officer you claim has wronged you IMMEDIATELY after you discover the wrong committed against you. Be ready to submit an Article 138 complaint immediately to your chain of command, in case the request for redress is refused.

e. The officer to whom you submitted the Article 138 complaint must promptly forward it to the officer exercising general court-martial jurisdiction, who is usually your commanding general (from here on, we'll assume this person is your commanding general for simplicity). Any commander through whom the complaint is forwarded may grant any redress within that particular commander's authority or may add pertinent material to the file and forward it to higher commanders. Upon receipt, the commanding general or a designated subordinate will examine your complaint. If the commanding general delegates the examination of the complaint to a subordinate, the subordinate must conduct an AR 15-6 investigation into the complaint, make a specific recommendation as to the appropriateness of the redress you have requested, and identify any other necessary corrective action. After the investigation, the commanding general must personally act on your complaint. He determines the merits of your complaint and grants or denies the redress you requested. If the commanding general believes redress is appropriate, but it is beyond his authority, he will forward your complaint to the agency or commander who has the authority to grant the redress. You will be notified in writing of the commanding general's action on your complaint. Your complaint and all supporting materials are then forwarded to Headquarters, Department of the Army (HQDA), along with the results of the commanding general's examination into your complaint and the action taken. At HQDA, the entire file is reviewed by The Judge Advocate General (or his designated representative) on behalf of the Secretary of the Army. The Judge Advocate General may return your file for additional information or further investigation. He may also recommend that the Secretary of the Army grant the redress you requested. You will be informed about the final disposition of your complaint by HQDA.

f. Your complaint is considered defective if:

(1) Your complaint deals with subject areas that are inappropriate for resolution under Article 138. The commanding general may look into your complaint to see if other channels are available for resolving the alleged wrong, but he will not make a decision or take action on the complaint.

(2) You fail to include all the information laid out above.

(3) You fail to submit a request for redress before submitting a formal Article 138 complaint. The commanding general may grant a waiver of deficiency under any of these circumstances in the interests of fairness and review the complaint as if it were properly prepared.

g. You may withdraw your Article 138 complaint at any time before final action is taken by HQDA. Your withdrawal of your complaint, however, must be completely voluntary. No person may order, direct, or demand that you withdraw your complaint, regardless of that person's rank, position, or authority. If this occurs, immediately consult with an attorney or the Inspector General's (IG) office. Your withdrawal may be accomplished by an oral request if you do it early enough, otherwise it must be in writing. The best way to withdraw your Article 138 complaint is to do it in writing, citing your complaint, the date you submitted it to your superior commissioned officer, and your desire to withdraw your complaint voluntarily and freely.

h. You have a right secured by The Uniform Code of Military Justice to submit an Article 138 complaint. Your chain of command may not take any retaliatory action against you. If you believe your chain of command is taking retaliatory action, see your attorney or consult with the IG's office. Do not take matters into your own hands -- let someone know about it and find out what you can do.

i. You have the right to consult with a legal assistance attorney for advice and assistance in drafting a request for redress and formal Article 138 complaint. You may also hire or consult with a civilian attorney at your own expense (no expense to the Government). A military attorney cannot represent you before any proceedings conducted under the provisions of AR 27-10 or Article 138, but a civilian attorney may do so.

j. An Article 138 complaint is a drastic action. It may consume a great deal of your time and energy, as well as that of your command. If at all possible, do your best to try to resolve the problem without going to the extent of submitting an Article 138 complaint. Don't be afraid to talk with your commander, first sergeant, or command sergeant major about the problem and how to resolve it. You may be pleasantly surprised at the results. However, if you have made reasonable and good faith efforts to resolve the problem and it has not worked, then look to the Article 138 complaint as a solution.

Appendix II

The Inspector General
Investigations Function

7-1. Inspector general investigations—purpose and procedures

a. Investigations as an inspector general function. Investigations is the IG function that provides the commander/directing authority another means through which to resolve allegations of impropriety. The primary purpose of IG investigations and investigative inquiries is to resolve allegations of impropriety efficiently and effectively by gathering evidence, evaluating the credibility of that evidence, analyzing that evidence in the context of identified standards, and packaging that analysis and subsequent conclusion in a well-written report. In this regard, IGs may investigate violations of policy, regulation, or law; mismanagement; unethical behavior; fraud; or misconduct. However, IGs will provide the command the opportunity to resolve allegations within command channels. Therefore, IGs will refer all command-appropriate allegations to the command in accordance with guidance from the directing authority or, if criminal in nature, to CID. Directing authorities should opt for an IG investigation or investigative inquiry when extreme discretion is necessary or when the command investigation is not likely to be efficient or effective. Once an IG initiates an investigation or investigative inquiry, the IG will complete the entire investigative action to determine if the allegations are "substantiated" or "not substantiated" (see para 7–2*b*, below) and if any issues are "founded" or "unfounded" (see para 6–1*a*, above).

(1) *Investigation.* A formal factfinding examination into allegations, issues, or adverse conditions of a serious nature that provides the directing authority a sound basis for making decisions and taking action. IG investigations involve the systematic collection and examination of evidence that consists of testimony recorded under oath; documents; and, in some cases, physical evidence. Only the directing authority can authorize IG investigations using a written and signed directive. IGs report the conclusions of their investigations using an ROI.

(2) *Investigative inquiry.* An informal factfinding examination into allegations, issues, or adverse conditions that are not significant in nature—as deemed by the command IG or the directing authority—and when the potential for serious consequences (such as potential harm to a Soldier or negative impact on the Army's image) are not foreseen. IG investigative inquiries involve

the collection and examination of evidence that consists of testimony or written statements; documents; and, in some cases, physical evidence. The directing authority reserves the right to direct an investigative inquiry if he or she feels an investigation or a command-directed investigation is not appropriate. Command IGs can only direct and approve investigative inquiries with written authority from the respective directing authority. IGs who resolve allegations using this methodology report their conclusions using an ROII.

b. The Inspector General action process. IGs will use the 7-step IGAP outlined in The Assistance and Investigations Guide to perform IG investigative inquiries and investigations. The guide is available from TIGS's website at https://tigs-online.ignet.army.mil/. The process outlined in the guide represents IG doctrine and is authoritative in nature; IGs may shape, tailor, and adapt the techniques and steps therein as necessary. The IG functions of assistance and investigations

56 AR 20–1 • 23 March 2020

share the IGAP, so IGs receiving complaints containing both issues and allegations often perform both functions concurrently. The prescriptive provisions to the process appear below:

(1) *Step 1, receive the inspector general action request.* The provisions in subparagraphs 6–1*d*(1)(*a*) through (c), above, apply.

(2) *Step 2, conduct inspector general preliminary analysis.* The provisions in subparagraphs 6–1*d*(2) (*a*) through (f), (h) through (j), and (l) apply. The following prescriptive measures also apply to this step of the IGAP when conducting investigations or investigative inquiries:

(a) IGs will promptly notify the next higher IG and the directing authority of any allegation that, if substantiated, would adversely affect public perception of the command, such as matters of media interest; complaints of sexual harassment; and reports of fraud, waste, and abuse.

(b) If the IG knows the complainant's identity, the IG must interview the complainant during this step or Step 4.

(c) The IG assigned to conduct the investigation will obtain a written directive from the directing authority (investigations only).

(3) *Step 3, initiate referrals and make initial notifications.* The provisions in subparagraphs 6–1*d*(3)(*a*) through (e), above, apply. The following prescriptive measures also apply to this step of the IGAP:

(a) IGs will inform complainants that the IG may refer any issues and allegations to the chain of command or other non-IG entity for resolution. Refusal by the complainant to consent to the release of relevant documentation may preclude the IG from resolving the complainant's issues. IGs will adhere to the records-

release provisions of chapter 3, above, when referring allegations to the chain of command.

(b) If the directing authority directs an IG investigation or investigative inquiry, the IG will verbally notify the subject's or suspect's commander or supervisor prior to conducting any interviews in that person's organization (except for the complainant interview, if necessary) and verbally notify the subject or suspect of the nature of the allegations before interviewing that person or requesting a statement.

(c) Record all notifications using the formats in The Assistance and Investigations Guide for later attachment to the ROI or ROII. The subject or suspect notification is evidence that the IG afforded the subject or suspect the right to know all allegations. The IG will record these notifications in the IGARS case notes.

(4) *Step 4, inspector general factfinding.* The following provisions for this step apply to investigations and investigative inquiries as specified.

(a) The IG will develop a written investigative plan that includes a witness list with the complainant, subject-matter experts, witnesses, and the subject or suspect; an interview sequence; and questions for each witness.

(b) (Required for investigations only but recommended for investigative inquiries): The IG will take recorded testimony under oath from all witnesses, subjects, and

suspects; make PA and FOIA notices; and render rights warnings for subjects and suspects with DA Form 3881 (Rights Warning Procedure/Waiver Certificate) when required in accordance with the guides and scripts contained in The Assistance and Investigations Guide. See paragraph 7–1*g* (2) for further guidance regarding subjects and the use of DA Form 3881.

(c) IGs will transcribe into written form, verbatim or summarized, all recorded testimony, taken under oath, for attach-ment as an exhibit in the ROI or, if applicable, the ROII. The IG will verify the accuracy of the written verbatim or summarized testimony against the recorded version before including it as an exhibit in the ROI or ROII. If portions of the recording prove difficult to hear or understand for technical or other reasons, the IG who conducted the interview will provide a supplemental memorandum summarizing those missed portions of the testimony.

(d) Persons who provide testimony in IG investigations and investigative inquiries and their legal counsel (if present) will not record their testimony by tape or other means in order to protect the confidentiality of witnesses, subjects, and suspects. Witnesses, subjects, and suspects may review their testimony for accuracy prior to completion of the investigation or investigative inquiry but will not alter the content. Clarifications, modifications, or additions to one's testimony will require a subsequent interview or a sworn, written statement at the investigating IG's discretion.

(e) IGs will ask people with whom they communicate during notifications and interviews not to disclose the matters under investigation or investigative inquiry, except their own personal counsel if they consult one without permission of the IG. IGs will not withhold permission for defense counsels to interview witnesses about matters under investigation, but IGs will not provide defense counsels with witness names due to IG confidentiality requirements.

(f) The IG will notify DAIG's Assistance Division within 2 working days of any subject, suspect, or witness who fails to answer a question or provide information during the course of an IG investigation or investigative inquiry if, in the IG's estimation, the individual's trustworthiness, reliability, and judgment in dealing with classified material comes into question. In such cases, TIG may notify the individual's commander to assess his or her continued access to classified material (see AR 380–67).

(g) The IG will capture the results of the investigation or investigative inquiry in an ROI, ROII, or hotline completion report (see para 7–2, below).

AR 20–1 • 23 March 2020 57

(h) The IG will obtain a written legal review of the ROI, ROII, or hotline completion report in memorandum or letter format if the report contains any substantiated allegations or resolves a complaint of statutory

whistleblower reprisal. The IG will include this legal review in the ROI or ROII, which should concur with the IG's substantiation of the allegation. Legal reviews are not required for ROIIs or hotline completion reports that do not contain substantiated findings.

(i) The IG will obtain the directing authority's approval for investigations and for investigative inquiries. The IG will upload the approved ROI/ROII, including all attachments, into the IGARS database.

(5) *Step 5, make notification of results.* The provision in subparagraph 6–1*d*(5), above, applies. The following prescriptive measures also apply to this step of the IGAP:

(a) The IG will notify the subject or suspect of the approved results of the investigation or investigative inquiry in writing (by return receipt if using the postal system), record that action in the IGARS database, and upload a copy of the notification in IGARS. The information in the database must accurately address the allegations, conclusions, recommendations, and command actions.

(b) As part of the written notification, the IG will explain to subjects or suspects with substantiated allegations or other unfavorable information the procedures necessary to obtain copies of the ROI or ROII under FOIA (see para 7–1*f*, below).

(c) The IG will notify the subject's or suspect's commander or supervisor of the approved findings. If

notifying any of these persons is inappropriate, the IG will notify a higher level commander of the results.

(d) Inspectors general will notify appropriate commanders of substantiated conclusions, even if the IG did not initially notify those commanders of the investigative inquiry or investigation. These notifications may be necessary when commanders change or when the subject or suspect has been assigned to a different command.

(e) IGs will notify subjects or suspects of any unfavorable information that the IG included in the ROI or ROII of which the subject or suspect was not initially apprised (see para 7–1*f,* below).

(f) IGs will maintain all notification records with the case file if the IG cannot attach the record to the electronic IGARS file.

(6) *Step 6, follow-up.* The following prescriptive measure applies to this step of the process. The IG will ensure that any responses from the subject or suspect to unfavorable information that will appear in the ROI or ROII are maintained with the hard copy case file if the IG cannot attach the record to the electronic IGARS file. Similarly, the IG will ensure that any notification of unfavorable information made to the subject or suspect, as opposed to unfavorable information made known and documented during the interview

process, is maintained with the case file if the IG cannot attach the notification to the electronic IGARS file.

(7) *Step 7, close the inspector general action request.* The provisions in subparagraphs 6–1*d*(7)(a) through (e), above, apply. The following prescriptive measure also applies to this step of the process: The IG will notify the complainant in writing, record the action in the IGARS database, and upload a copy of the notification in IGARS. The IG will maintain the notification record with the case file if the IG does not have access to IGARS or, due to connectivity problems, cannot upload the case and all supporting documents in IGARS.

c. Common guidelines with the assistance function. The guidance on command policy, general IG jurisdiction, time limits, emotional complainants, and so on outlined in paragraphs 6–1*c* through 6–1*f* and 6–3, above, apply to the investigations function. Additionally, refer to paragraphs 1–4*b*(5)(*e*) and 1–7*h*, above, for reporting and coordination guidance for allegations or issues related to classified information, sensitive activities, or SAPs.

d. Jurisdiction and directing authorities. The SECARMY has authorized TIG to investigate all Army activities. Only the SECARMY, the Under Secretary of the Army, the CSA, the VCSA, and TIG may direct DAIG investigations. Heads of HQDA agencies, commanders, and State AGs may request that TIG conduct an investigation, but they are not authorized to direct TIG to do so. TIG may direct a command IG at any level and in any Army component to conduct an investigation or investigative inquiry.

(1) IGs may investigate allegations against members of the command or subordinate commanders within the IG's sphere of activity as authorized by the directing authority.

(2) Command inspectors general may only direct and approve investigative inquiries within the IG's sphere of activity with written authority from the directing authority.

(3) The next higher IG will investigate allegations against the IG's commander unless that commander is a senior official. If the commander is a senior official, the IG will forward the allegation to DAIG's Investigations Division within 2 working days when practicable (see para 7–1*l*).

(4) Expanding the scope of an IG investigative or investigative inquiry, or adding additional allegations or individuals not originally addressed in the beginning of the investigation, requires the approval of the directing authority or command IG as applicable.

(5) If the IG discovers matters requiring investigative action that are unrelated or not subordinate to the allegations being addressed in the ongoing investigation or investigative inquiry, the IG will report

them to the directing authority or command IG for appropriate action. If the IG is not directed to investigate these new allegations, the IG will record them

58 AR 20–1 • 23 March 2020

in the "Other Matters" paragraph and recommend referral to the command or appropriate agency in the recommendations paragraph, both of which are found in the ROI or ROII. If these new allegations are resolved in the same investigation or investigative inquiry, the IG will document the genesis of the allegations in the background or introduction paragraph of the ROI or ROII.

(6) Inspectors general may conduct investigations and investigative inquiries at tenant units belonging to other ACOMs, ASCCs, and DRUs after coming to a mutual agreement between the IG who must conduct the investigation and the ACOM, ASCC, or DRU IG. Directing authorities at each level must be involved in this agreement process. DAIG's Assistance Division will resolve all jurisdictional issues.

(7) State AGs may direct IG investigations or investigative inquiries into Federal activities within their States, to include investigating matters concerning both the ARNG and ANG.

(8) Directing authorities may not terminate an IG investigation or investigative inquiry unless TIG approves.

e. Inspector general investigators. Only IGs may conduct IG investigations and investigative inquiries. IGs will actively lead these investigations with the assistance of assistant IGs, but assistant IGs may not conduct the investigation or investigative inquiry alone and unsupervised on behalf of an IG who may be leading the effort in name only. Actively leading the investigation or investigative inquiry means that the IG is participating in evidence-gathering and knows of all factfinding activities conducted by the assistant IG. When personnel are limited and the IG cannot be present for every interview, assistant IGs are authorized to administer the oath to a subject, suspect, and witness and conduct an interview without an IG present.

f. Unfavorable information. The IG must inform the subject or suspect of all unfavorable information that the IG includes in the final ROI or ROII and afford the subject or suspect an opportunity to respond prior to the final publication of the ROI or ROII. Unfavorable information is any derogatory information that reflects negatively on an individual's character, integrity, trustworthiness, or reliability. This information includes the allegations and any unfavorable information that the IG will include in the final ROI or ROII, including information contained in the "Other Matters" section. The IG may inform the subject or suspect orally or in writing. Once the IG has informed the subject or suspect, the IG must document this step and attach it to the ROI or ROII. Additionally, the IG can disclose evidence related to the unfavorable information to the subject or suspect if that evidence will aid the IG's factfinding effort. When disclosing such evidence, the IG must always take steps to protect confidentiality. No subject or suspect may be required to respond to unfavorable information. A subject or suspect who chooses to respond may do so by—

(1) Submitting to an interview by the IG.

(2) Providing a sworn, written statement.

(3) Submitting matters through the subject or suspect's attorney.

(4) Requesting that the IG consider certain documentary evidence.

(5) Requesting that the IG consider certain physical evidence.

(6) Requesting that the IG interview reasonably available witnesses with knowledge on the matter under investigation.

g. Rights of subjects, suspects, and witnesses. The rights of individuals in IG investigations and investigative inquiries depend upon their status as subjects, suspects, or witnesses. A subject is a person against whom noncriminal allegations have been made. A suspect is a person against whom criminal allegations have been made when the alleged acts are violations of punitive articles of the UCMJ, punitive sections of regulations, or other criminal laws. A witness is a person who saw, heard, knows, or has something relevant to the issues under investigation and who is not a subject or suspect. Subject-matter experts who impart to the IG their expertise are witnesses. A subject or a witness may become a suspect as a result of incriminating information that arises during an investigation or interview or whenever the IG believes the person has committed a criminal offense.

(1) Suspects—both Soldiers and Army Civilians—have the right to have a lawyer present when providing recorded testimony under oath (the lawyer may advise the suspect but not speak for him or her); the right to remain silent during questioning related to the matter; and the right to terminate the questioning. Accordingly, if suspects invoke their rights or fail to waive their rights after the IG properly advises them of such rights, the IG will record the time and terminate the interview without a read-out. Invoking one's rights and remaining silent does not constitute a failure to cooperate and cannot be the basis for any adverse or corrective action. Because the circumstances under which the IG may resume questioning are specific to the facts, the investigator will consult with the local legal office before initiating further discussions with these individuals (see UCMJ, Art 31 and Rules 304 and 305: Military Rules of Evidence (MRE)). When in doubt concerning these rules, the IG will consult with the servicing SJA or DAIG's legal advisor (SAIG–JA).

(2) Subjects—both Soldiers and Army Civilians—also have the right to remain silent during questioning related to the matter under investigation and have the right to terminate the questioning. The IG will notify the subject of this right during the pre-brief but will not administer a DA Form 3881. Accordingly, if a subject invokes his or her rights, or fails to waive those rights after the IG properly advises the individual of such, the IG will record the time and terminate the interview

AR 20–1 • 23 March 2020 59

without a read-out. Invoking one's rights and remaining silent does not constitute a failure to cooperate and cannot be the basis for any adverse or corrective action.

(3) Department of the Army personnel who are witnesses may not lawfully refuse to answer questions properly related to an IG investigation or investigative inquiry unless answering the question will incriminate them, will involve certain privileged communications (see para 7–1*h*, below), or will be in violation of their right to union representation as described in subparagraph *g*(3), below. However, if an IG suspects that a Soldier or Army Civilian under questioning has committed a criminal offense, the IG must advise that person of his or her rights under UCMJ, Art. 31 and 384 U.S. 436, as applicable.

(4) Any Army Civilian employee who belongs to a bargaining unit represented by a labor organization

certified as the exclusive representative of that unit has a right to union representation during IG subject or suspect interviews if the employee reasonably believes that the investigation may result in disciplinary action and the employee requests the representation. The local union contract may provide for union representation even when the employee does not request it. IGs will know the contents of the local union contract or will coordinate with the local CPAC management-employee relations specialist. If an Army Civilian employee serving as a witness is entitled to representation, and the witness requests a union representative, the IG must allow the representative to be present during the interview. During the interview, union representatives may comment, speak, or make statements but may not assume control, disrupt the proceeding, or answer for the interviewee. IGs will apply a standard of "reasonableness" when determining if a representative is being disruptive. The representative's presence is in addition to any right the employee may have to a lawyer. An IG must take every reasonable step to ensure that the representative can be present for the interview, such as granting extensions or notifying the union that the employee is having difficulty obtaining a representative.

h. Privileged evidence. IGs will not consider evidence that is privileged under the Manual for Courts Martial MRE as follows: communications between a lawyer and a client, privileged communications with clergy, the husband-wife communication privilege (except when the spouse uses government communications means), the political vote privilege, deliberations of courts and juries, and the psychotherapist-patient privilege. In addition, IGs will not use evidence derived from the illegal monitoring of electronic communications in violation of 18 USC 2511. Furthermore, IGs may not use in any IG investigation or investigative inquiry evidence derived from other evidence procured in violation of 18 USC 2511 pursuant to 18 USC 2515.

i. Allegations not appropriate for inspector general action. Several types of allegations are not appropriate for IG investigation or investigative inquiry as follows:

(1) *Serious criminal misconduct.* IGs will not investigate allegations of a nature that, if substantiated, would likely constitute serious criminal misconduct. Many allegations or acts of omission may appear as criminal insofar as they could be phrased as a dereliction of duty, violation of a regulation, or conduct unbecoming an officer, but that appearance does not necessarily preclude an IG investigation or investigative inquiry. IGs will coordinate or consult with the appropriate legal advisor in cases of this nature and with USACIDC officials if necessary.

(2) *Redress available through other means.* An IG will not ordinarily investigate allegations where established means of redress already exist to resolve such matters (see para 6–3*g,* above). Rather, IGs will only conduct due-process reviews for complainants who have

already used the established redress procedures but who feel that they did not receive due process.

(3) *Command investigations.*

(a) IGs will not investigate allegations when the command elects to resolve those matters using a commander's investigation or inquiry. IGs will always afford their commanders/directing authorities, or subordinate commanders who have the means to investigate, the opportunity to resolve the matter in command channels.

(b) The IG will formally refer all allegations to the command using a referral memorandum that includes the relevant information from the DA Form 1559 and associated continuation sheets, but the IG will not provide a copy of the DA Form 1559 and/ or its continuation sheets. If the command elects to investigate an allegation referred by the IG, the IG will await the command product before finalizing the allegation in the IG system. Command products include, but are not limited to, Rule for Courts-Martial 303 preliminary inquiries; Article 138: Uniform Code of Military Justice inquiries or investigations; and pre-liminary inquiries, administrative investigations, and boards of officers conducted under the provisions of AR 15–6. IGs will close out allegations investigated by the command in IGARS as "command referred" and not "substantiated" or "not substantiated." The IG will upload a copy of the referral in IGARS and

enter into the case notes the nature of the allegation received, the date referred to the command, the date the command accepted the referral, and the name of the complainant. Once the command completes the investigation, the IG will review the final command product to ensure that the command addressed the allegations and any related issues referred by the IG in a thorough and complete manner with findings supported by the evidence. If the command investigation addressed all referred allegations and issues, the IG will annotate in the synopsis the form of action the command took (for example, AR 15-6 investigation) and close the case in IGARS as "command referred." Whereas the IG may temporarily upload the command products in IGARS, the

60 AR 20-1 • 23 March 2020

IG will remove all command investigations or any other command products from the IGARS database (except those pro-vided by the complainant as evidence) prior to case closure.

(c) If the IG believes that the command investigation did not answer the allegations and issues referred by the IG, the IG will provide the responsible commander the opportunity to resolve the unanswered issues or allegations. If the commander and IG disagree about whether or not the commander addressed all allegations and issues referred by the IG, the IG will present the matter to the next higher commander for

action. If the next higher commander is the directing authority, the IG should obtain a legal opinion from the servicing legal office to assist in determining whether the command appropriately addressed the allegations and issues. The IG may recommend that the directing authority direct the investigating commander to conduct another investigation, direct the IG to investigate, or determine that the investigative actions taken were sufficient.

(d) If the directing authority directs the IG to investigate, the IG will complete an ROI or ROII and close the case in IGARS with a conclusion of "substantiated" or "not substantiated." If the directing authority determines that the investigating command did in fact answer all issues and allegations and the IG disagrees, the IG will annotate in the case notes the concerns regarding the unanswered allegations and issues, refer the matter in IGARS to the next higher IG office for review, and close the case in IGARS as "command referred." The immediate higher command IG will accept the referral to open a case in IGARS. If the higher command IG determines that the original command investigation answered all allegations and issues, the higher command IG will close the case in IGARS as "command referred." If the higher IG agrees with the referring IG, the higher IG will present the matter to his or her directing authority with a recommendation that the directing authority either initiate an investigation into the unanswered matters or direct the subordinate command to conduct an additional investigation into

those same matters. In either case, the IG should obtain a legal review from a servicing legal office agreeing that the command investigation did not address all the allegations or issues. If the directing authority determines that an additional investigation is not necessary, the IG will note the decision and close the case in IGARS as "command referred" (this requirement does not apply to DODIG Hotline Action cases or other cases in which DAIG is the OOR). TIG and DAIG's Assistance division chief, on behalf of TIG, can direct an investigation into matters even when the directing authority disagrees with his or her local IG.

(e) IGs who refer allegations and related issues to the command will provide as part of the command referral all relevant documentary evidence pertaining to the allegations and issues. The IG will inform the complainant or party providing the documentary evidence in writing that the allegations, issues, and the documentary evidence provided may be released to the command in unredacted form for a command investigation. The IG will obtain the document release form prior to initiating the referral to the command. The IG will protect, to the maximum extent possible, the confidentiality of the person(s) providing the documentary evidence. Refer to The Assistance and Investigations Guide for further details.

(f) These command-referral procedures also apply to cases received from DAIG's Assistance Division (SAIG–AC) as part of the DOD Hotline Program

outlined in DODI 7050.01. However, the IG must adhere to specific requirements when resolving allegations or issues presented in DOD Hotline cases. One of the requirements is that the IG will craft a Hotline Completion Report (HCR) for (1) all DOD action referrals, regardless of the findings made by the command, and (2) all information referrals supported by a command's inquiry / investigation resulting in a substantiated finding (see para 7–3*a*). Instead of a DA Form 1559, the IG will formally refer all allegations to the command using a referral memorandum based on the complaint submitted to the DOD Hotline and will then upload a copy of the referral in IGARS.

Note. For HCR reporting purposes, and in accordance with DODI 7050.01, an "allegation" is defined as a wrongdoing or impropriety that can be made against a person or a process. Consequently, all matters reported in an HCR will be crafted strictly as "allegations" and then documented as "substantiated" or "not substantiated."

(g) The IG will enter into case notes the nature of the allegation received, the date of referral to the command, the date the command accepted the referral, and the name of the complainant. Once the command completes the inquiry/investigation, the IG will review the command's final report product to ensure that the inquiry/investigation addressed all allegations and sufficiently met the standards outlined in DODI 7050.01. If the IG solely conducts an

investigation used as the sup-porting document for the HCR, then the IG must complete a "Quality Standards for Hotline Inquiries" statement formally confirming that his or her investigative actions met all of the quality standards listed in DODI 7050.01 and include it as a part of the command report, which the IG will verify. The IG will upload the statement, the command product, and the HCR into IGARS and submit it to DAIG's Hotline Branch. If the IG determines that the command investigation sufficiently addressed all IG-referred allegations, the IG will annotate that outcome in the synopsis. If the command product is found to be deficient (the IG identifies that the evidence does not support the findings, or the IG disagrees with the command product), then the IG will coordinate with the command to reconcile the deficiencies. If the IG believes the command did not satisfy the requirements and the identified deficiencies, the directing authority must take the actions necessary to re-solve them, or the IG may contact the chief of DAIG's Assistance Division, who, on behalf of TIG, can direct an investigation into allegations not adequately supported by evidence. The case will not be closed until DAIG, as the OOR, approves

AR 20–1 • 23 March 2020 61

the case for closure. The IG will upload all com-mand-product documents into the IGARS database whenever an HCR is prepared based on a com-mand investigation. Refer to The Assistance and

Investigations Guide for further details and how to code Hotline cases in IGARS.

(4) *Professional misconduct by an Army lawyer.* An IG will refer all allegations involving professional misconduct by an Army lawyer (military or civilian) through DAIG's legal advisor to the Senior Counsel having jurisdiction over the subject lawyer for disposition. Senior Counsels are the General Counsel of the Army, TJAG, the Command Counsel of the Army Materiel Command, or the Chief Counsel of the U.S. Army Corps of Engineers as defined in AR 27–26. The entire portion of the IG record that is relevant to the allegation against the lawyer will go to the Senior Counsel having jurisdiction over the subject lawyer (TIG's approval is not required). If the Senior Counsel intends to incorporate any part of the IG record into the final report, then TIG approval will be required. If an allegation does not present credible evidence that raises a substantial question about the lawyer's honesty, trustworthiness, or fitness to practice law, DAIG's legal advisor, after consultation with the Senior Counsel concerned (or that person's designated representative), may recommend the action be returned to the initiating IG without investigation by the Senior Counsel involved. In such circumstances, DAIG's Legal Advisor, in consultation with the IG who forwarded the case, will determine whether further action is warranted. Should a complaint of professional misconduct form the basis of a Whistleblower Reprisal allegation, the IG will contact DAIG's Legal Advisor.

Once the file has been transferred to the relevant Senior Counsel, it does not need to be returned to the IG, and there is no requirement, except to comply with DODIG's Hotline response provisions, for the legal chain of command to report the resolution of the claim to the IG.

(5) *Mismanagement in a Legal Office.* An IG will refer all allegations involving mismanagement in a legal office through DAIG's legal advisor to the Senior Counsel's designated representative to receive such complaints for disposition under applicable regulations. The entire portion of the IG record that is relevant to the allegation against the lawyer will go to the Senior Counsel's designated representative. TIG's approval is not required. If the Senior Counsel intends to incorporate any part of the IG record into the final report, then TIG's approval will be required. If the complaint does not present credible evidence of mismanagement in a legal office, DAIG's Legal Advisor, after consultation with the Senior Counsel's designated representative, may recommend the action be returned to the initiating IG without investigation by the Senior Counsel involved. In such circumstances, DAIG's Legal Advisor, in consultation with the IG who forwarded the case, will determine whether further action is warranted. Should a complaint of mismanagement form the basis of a Whistleblower Reprisal allegation, the IG will contact DAIG's Legal Advisor. Once the file has been transferred to the relevant Senior Counsel, it does not need to be returned to the IG, and there is no requirement, except

to comply with DODIG's Hotline response provisions, for the legal chain of command to report the resolution of the claim to the IG.

(6) *Professional misconduct by an Army chaplain.* IGs who receive allegations against Army chaplains regarding the quality of spiritual or religious counseling will open a case in IGARS, refer the allegations to the next higher supervisory chaplain, and then close the case in IGARS. If no clear higher headquarters for the chaplain is apparent, IGs will consult with the senior commander's chaplain's office. IGs will refer allegations concerning matters other than professional mis-conduct to the chain of command.

(7) *Civilian employee violations of the Hatch Act.* IGs will refer allegations of Civilian employee violations of the Hatch Act (5 USC 7322), limiting certain political activities of Federal employees, to the Office of Special Counsel (https://osc.gov).

j. Allegations requiring referrals to other inspectors general. Several types of allegations require prompt referral to other IGs as follows:

(1) *Allegations against inspectors general.* IGs will report all allegations against IGs (uniformed and Civilian) to the next higher echelon IG and to the ACOM, ASCC, or DRU IG for appropriate action within 2 working days after receipt. The ACOM, ASCC, or DRU IG will consult with DAIG's Assistance

Division to determine the best course of action to resolve the allegation. TIG retains the authority to investigate the allegation.

(a) If the allegations involve violations of AR 20–1 or other IG policy, the next higher IG, in coordination with DAIG's Assistance Division, will normally conduct the investigation or investigative inquiry.

(b) If the allegation deals with misconduct or other non-IG-related offenses, the command may relieve the IG for cause (or, in the case of Civilian IGs, suspend the IG from his or her duties temporarily or remove the individual) and use other investigative methods (such as an AR 15–6 investigation) or administrative actions to determine the facts of the case after coordinating with DAIG's Assistance Division.

(c) An IG will obtain an information copy of the approved ROI or inquiry (with the IGAR, allegation, and overall complaint attached) and forward it to both DAIG's Assistance Division and the ACOM, ASCC, or DRU IG con-currently with the report to the next higher echelon IG.

(d) Command IGs will notify TIG of any anticipated command or IG action before attempting to resolve the allegation.

62 AR 20–1 • 23 March 2020

(e) TIG may suspend the investigated IG's access to IGNET, IGARS, and all other IG information, including physical access to the IG office space within the command, until the allegation is resolved.

(2) *Professional misconduct by Army Healthcare Providers.* IGs do not investigate alleged professional misconduct (standard care/quality of care) by Army Healthcare Providers. These matters are a military treatment facility (MTF) responsibility in accordance with AR 40–68. Should the IG receive such a complaint, the IG's primary role is to open a case in IGARS, redirect the Soldier to the Patient Advocacy/Patient Experience Office at the MTF for redress in accordance with DODI 6000.14, and then close the case in IGARS. IGs will seek IG technical support from the U.S. Army Medical Command IG or the local servicing Regional Health Command IG for additional guidance and for appropriate procedures specific to the USAR/ARNG.

k. Allegations against any Army officer, noncommissioned officer, or enlisted Soldier.

(1) All Army IGs will enter into the IGARS database within 2 working days after receipt the complete name of the subject(s) or suspect(s) and the specific allegation(s) identified in any IGAR that has resulted in the initiation of an Army IG investigation or investigative inquiry against an Army enlisted Soldier, NCO, WO, commissioned officer (nonpromotable colonel and

below), or Army Civilian employee. This reporting requirement further applies to Army personnel serving in Joint and special assignments; Joint IGs in particular are required to report the initiation of an investigation against an Army member to DAIG's Assistance Division or Investigations Division by telephone or encrypted email, since Joint organizations will not have access to IGARS. Additional reporting requirements for allegations against colonels appear in paragraphs 1–4*b*(5)(*c*), above, and 7–1*l*(1), below.

(2) IGs will report to DAIG's Investigations Division within 2 working days after receipt any allegation presented to an Army IG against a colonel that will result in the same type of investigative action mentioned above, including those colonels serving in Joint and special assignments (for promotable colonels, see para 7–1*l*, below).

(3) Both law and policy require a review of IG records in conjunction with all senior official assignments, promotions, and retirements. Other IG records reviews are required for certain sensitive assignments and at the direction of senior Army leaders. DAIG's Records-Screening Division (SAIG-RSO) is the proponent for the screening of IG records in support of the Personnel Suitability Screening Program. The intent of these requirements is to ensure the selection of the best leaders and commanders, to consider information not available to the original board or in advance of the board, and to protect the rights of individuals.

l. Allegations against a senior official. Commanders, IGs, or principal HQDA staff officials must forward directly to DAIG's Investigations Division through IG channels any and all allegations of impropriety or misconduct (including criminal allegations) and complaints against senior officials—defined as general officers (including ARNGUS, USAR, and retired general officers), promotable colonels, PUSMAs, and SES Civilians—within 2 working days of receipt when practicable. Special Government employees (scientific or professional, senior level, defense intelligence senior level, and highly qualified experts) are considered senior officials and must also be reported. A National Guard colonel becomes a senior official when the officer is submitted to compete on a General Officer Federal Recognition Board (GOFRB) for a COE and remains a senior official until completion of the GOFRB process. Colonels selected by the GOFRB, confirmed by the Senate for a COE, and assigned to a general officer billet are considered senior officials. Colonels who receive a COE but are not assigned to a general officer billet are not considered senior officials until they are assigned to a general officer billet or nominated for a general officer billet. Forward all complaints to usarmy. pentagon.hqda-otig.mbx.saig-in-office@mail.mil or by commercial telephone at (703) 545–4545/4556. This reporting requirement also includes any other conduct of reasonable concern or significance to the Army or DOD leadership, especially when the alleged misconduct includes an element of misuse of position or of unauthorized personal benefit to the senior official, a Family member, or an associate.

(1) IGs will record all referrals of allegations against senior officials in the IGARS database in accordance with the guidance outlined in The Assistance and Investigations Guide. Inspectors general will not conduct any fact-finding into the nature of the allegations unless authorized by TIG, DTIG, or the chief of DAIG's Investigations Division.

(2) Only the SECARMY, the Under Secretary of the Army, the CSA, the VCSA, and TIG may authorize or direct an investigation or investigative inquiry into allegations of improprieties or misconduct by a senior official or an individual of equivalent grade or position. As a matter of Army policy, when such allegations are suspected against a senior official or discovered during a non-IG investigation or inquiry (such as a commander's inquiry, an AR 15–6 investigation, or CID investigation), the commander or command concerned will halt the inquiry or investigation and report the allegations within 2 working days to DAIG's Investigations Division (SAIG–IN) for further action. As a specific exception, EEO and Anti-Deficiency Act inquiries or investigations may continue even if they involve senior officials as long as DAIG's Investigations Division has been notified.

(3) IGs who receive allegations against senior officials may tell their commanders the general nature of the

allegations and the identity of the person against whom the allegations were made—but only after contacting DAIG's Investigations

AR 20–1 • 23 March 2020 63

Division for advice. An open investigation may already exist, and DAIG's Investigations Division may have already in-formed the commander. To protect the complainant's confidentiality, the IG will not reveal either the source or specific nature of the allegations. TIG will ensure that the appropriate commanders; the ACOM, ASCC, or DRU IG; the Chief, Army Reserve; and the CNGB, receive addi-tional information as appropriate.

(4) If the IG who receives the allegation works for the subject of the allegation, or if questions arise, the IG will contact DAIG's Investigations Division for guidance and to allow DAIG to contact the commander and avoid an ethical dilemma for the IG.

(5) IGs or commanders will forward allegations against PMs or PEOs who are senior officials to DAIG's Investigations Division within 2 working days. If the allegations are against the PM or PEO staff, the IG of the supporting LCMC will normally resolve the allegations. The LCMC IG will inform the PM or PEO of the general nature of the allegations; the identity of the person against whom the allegations were made; and, upon the investigation or investigative inquiry's

completion, the conclusions when appropriate. Final ROI or ROII approval rests with the directing authority.

(6) Questions should be addressed to DAIG's Investigations Division at the U.S. Army Inspector General Agency (SAIG–IN), 1700 Army Pentagon, Room 1E115A, Washington, DC 20310–1700 via email at usarmy.pentagon.hqda-otig.mbx.saig-in-office@mail.mil or by commercial telephone at (703) 545–4545/4556 or to DAIG's legal advisor at USAIGA (SAIG–JA), 1700 Army Pentagon, Room 1E132, Washington, DC 20310–1700.

m. Allegations involving minor infractions. IGs must use judgment when determining whether or not an allegation represents a minor infraction. The IG must make this determination during step 2, inspector general preliminary analysis, of the IGAP to determine if an allegation represents a minor infraction on its face or, after analyzing the complaint, rises to the level of an impropriety requiring an IG or command-level investigation (see para 7–1*d*(2)(b)). Designating an alle-gation as a minor infraction depends upon the judgment of the IG. However, all minor infractions must be non-punitive in nature. Examples of minor infractions include inappropriate wear of the uniform (but not the wearing of unauthorized awards), parking a privately owned vehicle in the wrong location, failing to return a salute, and so on. Minor infractions will not include alleged incidents as described by the complainant during step 1, receive the inspector general action request, in which the subject may have received personal benefit; there was detriment to others; there was waste of govern-ment time, resources, personnel, or money; and / or there was an improper personal relationship (personal or official). IGs may resolve minor infractions through teaching and training and often in consultation with the directing authority or sub-ordinate chain of command. In each case, the command IG will approve any designation of an allegation as a minor infraction. This provision is not a license for IGs to reject allegations out of hand. The IG must be able to defend why he or she considered the infraction to be minor and document that rationale in the IGARS database.

7–2. Reports of investigation and investigative inquiry

a. Requirements. IGs will resolve all allegations by completing an ROI for an investigation and an ROII for an investigative inquiry that provides a clear, complete, objective, and impartial analysis of all pertinent evidence gathered. IGs will include in the ROI or ROII all copies of documents that the IG considered as evidence. The IG will follow the formats for ROIs or ROIIs provided in The Assistance and Investigations Guide.

b. Conclusions. All IGs will use the investigative con-clusions outlined below for all issues and allegations contained in ROIs and ROIIs. These conclusions will contain the specific allegation(s) and issue(s) and state that the allegation or issue occurred (substantiated or founded respectively) or did not occur (not substantiated or unfounded respectively). These conclusions will establish IG findings regarding violations by a specific individual of an established standard and will not be vague statements.

(1) IGs will use the conclusion of "substantiated" when a preponderance of credible evidence, as viewed by a reason-able person, exists to support the allegation.

(2) IGs will use the conclusion of "not substantiated" when a preponderance of credible evidence, as viewed by a reasonable person, does not exist to support the allegation.

(3) IGs will use the term "founded" for issues contained in the ROI or ROII that accompanied the allegation(s) to show that the issues had merit and required resolution (see para 6-1*a*, above).

(4) IGs will use the term "unfounded" for issues contained in the ROI or ROII that accompanied the allegation(s) to show that the issues lacked merit and did not require resolution (see para 6-1*a*, above).

(5) IGs will not use conclusions such as "the allegation was not substantiated, founded, or refuted" or phrases such as "partially substantiated," "partially founded," or "substantiated in part."

(6) Inspectors general who close cases administratively or decline them will code those cases as assistance in IGARS and clearly identify this fact in the synopsis and case notes, to include the authority for the action. IGs will enter the complaint as an issue and will not enter a subject, suspect, or allegation.

(7) IGs will use the phrase "closed without findings" when the investigation or investigative inquiry is terminated prior to conclusion due to the following special circumstances:

64 AR 20–1 • 23 March 2020

(a) The allegation concerns actions more than 3 years old. The IG will document the relevant time period and close the case without findings.

(b) A legal process such as a court order or a settlement between the U.S. Government and a subject and/or complainant includes a requirement to terminate all ongoing inquiries or investigations. The IG will obtain a copy of the order or settlement, include it in the case file, and record the matter as "closed without findings."

(c) The Inspector General approves termination of an investigation or investigative inquiry (see para 7–1*d*(8), above).

c. Recommendations. An IG will not recommend adverse action against an individual in an ROI, ROII, or hotline completion report, except for whistleblower cases as discussed below. Commanders who contemplate requesting to use the IG product for such action must balance the possible adverse consequences on the IG as a fair and impartial fact-finder and possible due process rights of the individual that may require release of confidential testimony, personal information, and deliberative material (opinions, conclusions, and recommendations). An IG may recommend administrative action to correct a mistake (for example, recovery of an improper temporary duty payment). In all cases, IGs will recommend to "close the case" or "turn the case over to a follow-on investigator." In cases of substantiated whistleblower reprisal allegations, IGs will make specific recommendations in accordance with the examples in The Assistance and Investigations Guide and recommend forwarding the report for appropriate consideration for the responsible management official identified.

d. Processing. Inspectors general will process all ROIs, ROIIs, and hotline completion reports as follows:

(1) Command IGs will ensure the directing authority is aware of—and familiar with—the ROI, ROII, or hotline completion report approval and notification process. Directing authorities will approve all ROIs unless a deputy commander is designated to do so in writing. The directing authority may also reserve the right

to approve ROIIs or hotline completion reports with substantiated allegations. However, command IGs can approve ROIIs consistent with written authority from the directing authority. Command IGs will also notify the directing authority if the IG substantiates the allegation.

(2) Prior to approval, the command IG will forward the completed ROI, ROII, or hotline completion report to the supporting SJA or command counsel to conduct a legal sufficiency review. Legal reviews are required for all ROIIs or hotline completion reports with substantiated findings and all ROIs regardless of the findings. Once the legal sufficiency review concurring with the substantiated findings is complete, the command IG will forward all ROIs to the directing authority for approval.

(3) The directing authority or command IG (depending on the methodology used and guidance provided by the directing authority) will approve or disapprove the report in its entirety or in part and sign the report to indicate approval or disapproval. If the directing authority disapproves the IG ROI, the IG must work with the directing authority to resolve the disapproval by conducting additional investigative actions as necessary in order to obtain approval. If the IG is unable to resolve the disapproval, the IG should contact the next higher IG and/or the Assistance Division for guidance. Once ap-proved, the directing authority will then take action on the approved portions that are within the authority

and responsibility of the directing authority. For whistleblower reprisal and DOD Hotline cases, a record of these actions in memorandum form will be attached to the final report and all subsequent copies.

(4) The IG will forward through IG channels to the next higher commander an ROI, ROII, or hotline completion report, or any portion of the ROI, ROII, or hotline completion report, complete with recommendations, that requires action at levels above that of the directing authority. Each higher commander will indicate approval or disapproval and take appropriate action on matters within their authority to affect. IGs will forward remaining matters through IG channels, with appropriate recommendations, to the command echelon best suited to address those matters.

(5) When TIG directs an investigation, the immediate commander of the IG who conducted the investigation will indicate concurrence or nonconcurrence of the investigation's conclusions. The IG will then forward the report through IG channels to TIG. As the directing authority and IG OOR, TIG has final approval authority of the report.

Dear Readers,

Congratulations on completing this essential guide to navigating and overcoming toxic leadership in your workplace! As someone who has experienced the challenges of toxic environments firsthand, I understand the complexities and frustrations that can arise.

You've taken the first step towards reclaiming your work environment from toxicity. Together, let's continue this journey of empowerment and resilience. It's time to equip ourselves with the tools and strategies to identify, manage, and overcome toxic leadership.

To connect with a supportive community of individuals who share your experiences and commitment to overcoming workplace challenges, follow me on Instagram @AuthorJasonPike and Facebook @Jason-Pike, or visit my website www.JasonPike.org.

Thank you for embarking on this journey with me. Let's stand united in our pursuit of healthier, more supportive workplaces.

Lt. Col. Jason G. Pike, USA, Retired
www.JasonPike.org

About The Author

Adecorated combat veteran with multiple deploy-ments, Lt. Col. Jason G. Pike, USA, Retired, served 31 years in the United States Army as both an enlisted and officer, including nine years overseas in five coun-tries. Jason earned over 30 service awards & badges and survived a wicked amount of military training.

His first book, *A Soldier Against All Odds*, compiles all his life events in an inspiring storytelling format with the ups and downs of a life in uniform. His diversity of

Army jobs, assignments, and schools from age 17 to 48 sets this military memoir up differently than most.

Jason's brutal honesty on how he did it while disclosing many sacred secrets about how he survived is unique. With a straightforward account of one man's journey, he inspires audiences nationwide at speaking events and shows how to be resilient and to persevere no matter what disadvantages and life struggles may happen.

After having walked through the VA benefits bureaucracy and endless paperwork, Pike has made it his business to master getting the benefits he earned, and he now has a much-needed blueprint to help other veterans do the same. His second book, *Out of the Uniform, Back into Civilian Life*, is an invaluable resource for veterans seeking clear, actionable guidance to navigate the often complex landscape of VA benefits and assistance programs.